Struggle for Justice

A STORY OF THE AMERICAN COMMITTEE
FOR THE INDEPENDENCE OF ARMENIA
1915–1920

Frontispiece image: *Boundary between Turkey and Armenia as Determined by Woodrow Wilson, President of the United States of America.* (Scale 1:1,000,000.) The map was compiled in 1920 under the direction of Major Lawrence Martin of the General Staff of the U.S. Army by the topographic branch of the U.S. Geological Survey in cooperation with the Department of State.

Struggle for Justice

A STORY OF THE AMERICAN COMMITTEE
FOR THE INDEPENDENCE OF ARMENIA
1915–1920

Robert George Koolakian

Armenian Research Center
University of Michigan-Dearborn
Dearborn, Michigan
2008

Cataloging-in-Publication Data

Koolakian, Robert G.
Struggle for justice: a story of the American Committee for the Independence of Armenia, 1915-1920 / Robert George Koolakian.
155 p. : ill., facsim., map ; 28 cm.
Includes bibliographical references and index.
ISBN: 1-934548-00-6
ISBN13: 978-1-934548-00-4
1. Armenian massacres, 1915-1923—Foreign public opinion, American.
2. Azadian, Harutun Bab, d. 1965.
3. United States—Relations—Armenia.
4. Armenians—New York (State)—Syracuse—History.
5. Near East Relief (Organization).
6. American Committee for the Independence of Armenia.
DS195.5.K66 2008
956.6'20156—dc22

The paper used in this publication meets the minimum requirements of the American National Standard for Information Sciences-Permanence of Paper for Printed Materials, ANSI Z39.48-1984.

This volume was edited by Mary Beth Hinton, William T. La Moy designed it, and Michele Combs provided its index.

IMAGE ON THE FRONT COVER: fig. 60 on page 118. View of the banquet head table at the first convention of the American Committee for the Independence of Armenia, Hotel Plaza, New York, Saturday, 8 February 1919.

IMAGE ON THE BACK COVER: fig. 59 on page 117. Overview of the banquet at the first convention of the American Committee for the Independence of Armenia, Hotel Plaza, New York, Saturday, 8 February 1919.

MAJOR SPONSORS

Paula Boghosian
Charles and Judy, Cyndi, Kim, and Heather Koolakian
Richard Roomian
Violet Margosian
Chuck and Tulie, and Georganna and Charles Jr. Yessaian

FRIENDS OF THE KOOLAKIAN BOOK PROJECT

Diane Yessaian Costa
Charles Sarkis Costa
Alice Nigoghosian, in memory of Agnes O. Nigoghosian
Sandra S. Nigoghosian, in memory of Sirabion Nigoghosian
Zarm Taft

We cannot ignore the public responsibility engendered by the Armenian massacres. The condition appeals to the civility of every respectable American and it goes to the heart of each and every one who entertains fairness of thought toward the treatment of an innocent God-fearing race. I cannot help thinking that there is more to the Armenian question than the mistreatment of a minority people. Surely these are crimes against all of humanity and they place a heavy burden upon the conscience of the western world. It is fitting that Americans should help the Armenians in their hour of need. I know of no cause more worthy, nor effort more dignified.

Alice Stone Blackwell
American Board of Commissioners for Foreign Missions
20 October 1917

"Remember the Armenian Massacre"

In the years 1915–18 when . . . the mass deportation and annihilation of a whole people could still shock Americans . . . American missionaries didn't keep silent. . . . They urged the State Department to intervene. It was a different State Department then; it did.

[William Jennings Bryan] the American Secretary of State at the time . . . not only had convictions but expressed them. He protested these massacres vociferously—"as a matter of humanity."

The American Ambassador to Turkey, Henry Morgenthau, did what he could to publicize this first genocide of the century even before there was a name for a crime so huge. He saw to it that the whole world knew of the plight of the Armenians. Ambassador Morgenthau's conclusion: "If America is going to condone these offenses . . . she is party to the crime."

Theodore Roosevelt made the same point, demanding a declaration of war against Turkey when the massacres came to light.

Even today some [elder] Americans may remember being told to think of "the starving Armenians" when they were children and wouldn't eat their vegetables. The phrase remains in the language even if the history behind it has been forgotten.

[Paul Greenberg, excerpted from "Remember the Armenian Massacre," *Syracuse Herald-American*, 5 November 2000.]

Contents

Illustrations

Note that, unless otherwise indicated, all illustrations are from the papers of Harutun Azadian and George Koolakian, which are in the author's possession.

Robert Koolakian has produced this book as a labor of love. Having inherited from his grandfather George Koolakian a cache of unique documents that illuminate the post–World War I Armenian independence movement in the United States, he undertook to share these documents and place them in historical context. I commend his effort.

When, some years ago, Mr. Koolakian brought these materials to my home, my wife and I were quite impressed by the numerous telegrams that the elder Koolakian and his colleagues had received from Washington, D.C., especially those bearing the signature of President Woodrow Wilson. A photograph of a large banquet, held in 1919 at the Plaza Hotel in New York City, revealed the presence on that occasion of many influential and famous individuals. They had gathered to inaugurate a movement to establish a free and independent Armenia that would be closely tied to the United States, perhaps as a United States mandate, and their meeting resulted in the American Committee for the Independence of Armenia.

Alas, the movement was short-lived. The interest of America's elite in the independence of Armenia was high until mid-1920, when it began to drop precipitously. This rapid change was no doubt due to the unexpected takeover by the Bolsheviks of Caucasian Armenia and the realization that historic Armenia had been denuded of its indigenous Armenian inhabitants by the genocide carried out by the Young Turk government and its immediate successors from 1915 to 1923.

By early 1921, many leaders in the United States were prepared to put the Armenian genocide behind them, and in 1923, they were eager to seek concessions from the newly established Turkish Republic. America's leadership never looked back. It is only through the efforts of the Armenian community in the United States that the issue of the Armenian genocide has been kept before the public. Otherwise, the United States state department considers the Republic of Turkey an indispensable ally.

I recommend Koolakian's book to the general reader and to those who love to learn about the history of upstate New York, particularly that of the city of Syracuse. They will find in this work a trove of interesting materials concerning the period from the 1890s, when the first Armenians arrived there, to 1920. I encourage scholars to examine Koolakian's archival materials for the light they shed on the fate of Armenia and on America's involvement in that fate.

Serious historians rarely look at the "what might have been" in history. However, it is almost impossible not to dream of the once-real possibility that the United States would accept a mandate over Armenia. If that had happened, Armenia would now have a thriving economy and enjoy the closest and most cordial relations with the United States. Robert Koolakian's book opens up that beautiful vista, if only for a fleeting moment.

Dennis R. Papazian, Professor of History, Emeritus
Former Director, Armenian Research Center
University of Michigan-Dearborn

It is often said that our earliest impressions are ones that remain with us for a lifetime. This is certainly true of my early memories of my grandfather George Koolakian and his close friends Harutun Azadian and Harry Philibosian. However, in those days, I did not comprehend the nature and significance of the role these men played in the first Armenian independence movement in America during the early years of the twentieth century.

This account is a product of many years of research that began with the preparation of my graduate thesis, "Mr. Azadian Came to America," written while I was apprenticed at the New York State Historical Association at Cooperstown. Although many individuals and organizations contributed to this project, I, of course, remain responsible for any flaws or weaknesses in the final product.

I am indebted to Frank Rupp of the Syracuse Masonic Temple, who provided valuable information about the Syracuse "triumvirate" of Harutun Azadian, George Koolakian, and Harry Philibosian. Alice Murphy of the Syracuse and Onondaga County Americanization League related the history of her organization and its early connection with the American Committee for Armenian and Syrian Relief (ACASR) in central New York. Evamaria Hardin, an upstate New York architectural historian, translated Azadian family documents from the German. I am indebted to Agnes (Aghavni) Nigoghosian for many translations rendered from various documents and letters written in Armenian.

James H. Tashjian, former editor of the *Armenian Review,* shared his detailed study of primary documents in the Vahan Cardashian Collection, which shed light on many Azadian and Koolakian holdings. Dr. Tashjian also improved my understanding of the relationship that Azadian, Koolakian, and Philibosian had with the American Board of Commissioners for Foreign Missions (ABCFM) and Near East Relief (NER). Arpena S. Mesrobian, former director of the Syracuse University Press, spent many hours reviewing the Azadian and Koolakian memorabilia and provided information about early Armenian settlers in central New York. Richard C. Robarts, president of the Near East Foundation, related the early history of that organization and identified connections between NER documents and those of Azadian and Koolakian.

I am greatly indebted to Alice Nigoghosian, former associate director of the Wayne State University Press in Detroit for her guidance throughout the various stages of my work. Paula Der Boghosian, formerly on the faculty of Cazenovia College, evaluated the Azadian and Koolakian papers more than ten years ago, which prompted their later organization while preparing the initial manuscript copy in typed format. Gerald E. Ottenbreit, editorial assistant at the University of Michigan Armenian Research Center, devoted many hours to this project. Dick Case of the *Syracuse Post-Standard,* a longtime friend and colleague from our Cooperstown graduate program days, provided valuable comments and suggestions throughout its preparation.

Four people secured the future of the Azadian holdings as a working study collection: Arshalouis Azadian Randall, daughter of Harutun B. Azadian; her attorney, Crandall Melvin Jr. of Syracuse; and the executors of her estate, Carlton and Mary Lou Straub of Rochester, New York.

The following people have been helpful in various ways: Levon Avdoyan of the Library of Congress, Jordan Tsolakides, Richard Hovannisian, Edmond Azadian, Ara Sanjian, Henry Morgenthau III, Vahakn Dadrian, Max Boudakian, Ron Suny, Jane Hoehner, Dickran Kouymjian, Helen (Koolakian) and Azad H. Minasian, Arshalouis (Azadian) and Dorus P. Randall, Emma (Azadian) Cargen, Eleanor (Azadian) Jones, Antaram Desteian, Ardemis Desteian, and Richard H. Roomian.

From the Maxwell School of Citizenship and Public Affairs, I am indebted to Ambassador Goodwin Cook, David Bennett, and Peter Marsh, whose early advice and guidance assisted the initial study and approach to this volume.

From the College of Arts and Sciences at Syracuse University, Ruth Benedict, Kandice Salomone, and their staff, were very helpful. Syracuse University archivist Edward Galvin, as well as Sean Quimby, director of the Special Collections Research Center and his staff, also deserve my thanks.

Mary Beth Hinton edited the text, William La Moy designed the volume, and Michele Combs provided the index.

Finally, warmest thanks are given to my brother, Charles E. Koolakian, formerly president of Koolakian's of Syracuse, who secured the earliest occupational records of the family clothing store among the many effects of its founder, George G. Koolakian, our grandfather. The personal and professional memorabilia from his company during its formative years in the United States from 1905 to 1920 have confirmed some of the most important research and documentation pertaining to the main thrust of this story: his association with the American Board of Commissioners for Foreign Missions, his involvement in the earliest work of the American Committee for Armenian and Syrian Relief/Near East Relief, and his participation in the founding activities of the American Committee for the Independence of Armenia from 1918 to 1920.

R. G. K.
October 2007

For Dad and Mom,

HAIG AND NAZIK KOOLAKIAN,

for their gentle but persistent encouragement, their appreciation of history, and for knowing to put things away for a future day.

INTRODUCTION

At the close of World War I, a group of prominent Americans met at the head-quarters in Manhattan of the American Committee for Armenian and Syrian Relief (ACASR). The ink was hardly set on the armistice when this meeting took place in mid-November 1918. Three of the committee's trustees, James L. Barton, Cleveland H. Dodge, and William Wheelock Peet, sent a formal petition to Woodrow Wilson recommending the creation of the organization that would become the American Committee for the Independence of Armenia (ACIA).[1] Within a few days, their petition arrived at the United States state department, which forwarded it to the White House on 22 November—just in time to accompany the president on his way to the Paris Peace Conference.

From its inception in November 1918, the ACIA's development was guided by the state department and the ACASR, in collaboration with the United States armed forces, the War Industries and the Naval Consulting boards, the war department, and the United States attorney general's office. During the next two and one-half months, the state department enlisted support for the new organization from Allied (and some neutral) nation officials and representatives from Great Britain, France, Italy, Sweden, Greece, China, and Japan; many of them were involved in the earliest meetings of the ACIA.

The ACIA founding ceremonies, which took place in Manhattan from Friday, 7 February, through Tuesday, 11 February 1919, were among the most auspicious peacetime gatherings in modern history. The main event, a banquet at the Hotel Plaza, was attended by more than four hundred people, including past and future United States presidents and their families; state and territorial governors; United States cabinet, House, Senate, and state department representatives; prominent news people; engineers; scientists; actors; authors; educators; composers; recording artists; lawyers; industrialists; financiers; religious leaders; medical personnel; Allied military leaders; and social reformers, as well as delegates to the Paris Peace Conference.[2] The occasion—indeed the Armenian independence movement itself—had gained top-level visibility and international support.

Available evidence suggests that the following people were among those present: Douglas Haig, Henri Philippe Pétain, Robert E. Peary, Alfred E. Smith, William Howard Taft, Henry Cabot Lodge, Henry Morgenthau Sr., Bernard M. Baruch, Josephus Daniels, Mark Lambert Bristol, Victor Herbert, John D. Rockefeller, F. Scott Fitzgerald, Rudolph Valentino, Clarence Darrow, Andrew Mellon, J. Pierpont Morgan Jr., William Jennings Bryan, Calvin Coolidge, Warren G. Harding, Owen D. Young, Irving Berlin, William Randolph Hearst, Alice Stone Blackwell, Charles Evans Hughes, Nicholas Murray Butler, Willa Cather, Stephen S. Wise, George Eastman, Jane Addams, and Madeleine (Mrs. John Jacob) Astor.

George G. Koolakian, the ACASR-ACIA liaison, kept a photograph (see fig. 59 on page 117) of the banquet that was found among the effects of his son and daughter-in-law, Haig and Nazik Koolakian, after their deaths. That banquet proved to be the culmination of the brief, although important, story of the American Committee for the Independence of Armenia.

CHAPTER ONE
THE ARMENIAN PLIGHT AND THE AMERICAN REACTION

An unprecedented outpouring of humanitarian relief from America and Europe followed the 1915 Armenian massacres. However, Turkish atrocities against Armenians were not new. Many older Americans saw the connection between current events and the massacres of the Armenians in the 1890s in which an estimated two hundred thousand innocent victims had lost their lives. Even though some twenty years separated these tragic events, both resulted from the attempt to displace and destroy an ancient indigenous population, in the latter instance under the cover of war.

Who were the Americans who reacted to the first genocide of the twentieth century, and why were they involved in supporting the Armenian independence movement in the months immediately following World War I? They were members of the American Board of Commissioners for Foreign Missions (ABCFM) and the American Committee for Armenian and Syrian Relief/ Near East Relief (ACASR/NER).

Established in Boston in 1810, the ABCFM had done missionary work in the Ottoman Empire since the 1820s.[3] Although their attempts to Westernize the Muslim population had been a complete failure, by mid-century, they had gained a significant presence throughout the empire. Their efforts to aid the Christian minorities in Constantinople gave rise to the worldwide Armenian evangelical movement, with the founding of the Armenian Protestant Mission Church at Pera in 1846. The ABCFM established schools, hospitals, orphanages, and colleges of higher learning throughout many urban areas and provinces of the empire. The missionaries were thus positioned to chronicle social and political conditions.

Upon the occasion of their seventy-fifth anniversary, the trustees of the Near East Foundation recalled the birth of their predecessor organizations, the American Committee for Armenian and Syrian Relief (ACASR) and Near East Relief (NER):

> The Near East Foundation has its roots in the first large-scale refugee crisis of the twentieth century. In 1915, as the outbreak of World War I caused violent upheavals in the Ottoman Empire, countless numbers of Armenians, Greeks and other minorities in the Near East were forced from their homes and were dying from hunger, disease, and exposure. In early September, responding to a plea from U.S. Ambassador Henry Morgenthau, a group of distinguished Americans met in New York City and quickly agreed that urgent relief measures were needed to help these innocent victims survive the coming winter in the Anatolian countryside. Convened by Cleveland H. Dodge, this original committee included such people as James L. Barton, Charles Crane, Stephen Wise, and Samuel L. Dutton, who among them had decades of experience in the Middle East and a deep concern for the people of this region.

Within a month, the committee met its initial pledge of one hundred thousand dollars, and the funds were forwarded to Ambassador Morgenthau to feed, shelter, and clothe the refugees. Even as this effort was initiated, it became clear that the problem was of devastating proportions and demanded a longer-term commitment. Taking up this challenge, the original group, organized as the American Committee for Armenian and Syrian Relief, continued to raise funds for the refugees—collecting and distributing over twenty-five million dollars during the war years. Hundreds of thousands of refugees were fed, clothed, housed, and cared for in camps in Turkey, Syria, Lebanon, the Caucasus, and Persia. Although the original appeal for relief came on behalf of the Christian minorities, help was given to all suffering people on the basis of "need, not creed." Despite the scope of its work, the committee continued during this early period to function in a fairly informal manner. None of the money so desperately needed abroad was used to promote the fund-raising campaigns; members of the committee served as volunteers and covered all administrative costs; and publicity for the cause of relief in the Near East was generated by events as they unfolded in the region.

After the armistice, the committee saw the magnitude of the problem as so great, and the momentum to help so strong, that the effort was expanded and organized on a more permanent basis. In 1919, the committee was chartered by an act of Congress as Near East Relief and designated as the primary channel for United States postwar aid in the region. The new organization immediately launched a campaign to raise thirty million dollars to continue assistance for refugees unable to return to their homes. "Hunger Knows No Armistice" became the rallying cry for this campaign. Each town and city in the United States was asked to contribute an amount based on its population; by 1921, less than two years after its inception, the thirty-million-dollar goal was reached.

Much more than money was involved in the work of Near East Relief. Hundreds of American doctors, nurses, and social workers were recruited to staff clinics, schools, and shelters throughout the Near East. Tons of clothing were collected in NER's New York warehouse and shipped overseas. This direct relief soon gave way to "relief through giving work," and the idea of training people for a better life was born. Orphans and refugee women made embroideries and rugs that were sold all over the United States; all proceeds went to NER's overseas work. Orphanage workshops produced most of the clothing for the orphans. Hundreds of thousands of boys and girls—orphans or [children] separated from their families—were housed, fed, and taught practical skills by a corps of dedicated teachers. As they completed training and reached the age of sixteen, these young people were placed in jobs, and large-scale "matching" programs were organized to attempt to reunite them with the remnants of their families. More than a million displaced adults were also taught skills to help them adapt to their new lives.

In an outpouring of generosity unprecedented in the annals of private philanthropy, ordinary people in the United States reached out to help the victims of war and persecution in the Near East. In homes, schools, churches, and clubs across the United States, millions of Americans responded to the plea to "remember the starving Armenians."

For its role in giving these people a chance to live useful lives, NER has been credited with saving a whole generation of Armenians.[4]

The ABCFM had recorded internal skirmishes and massacres during the Crimean War and again in 1860, as well as those occurring since Sultan Abdul Hamid II's rise to the Ottoman throne in 1876. By the 1890s, the ABCFM realized that the Ottoman government had no intention of implementing reforms favorable to the Armenians that were promised at the 1878 Congress of Berlin, which followed the Russo-Turkish War of 1877 and 1878. Instead, the Turkish administrators were planning and carrying out pernicious deeds.[5] The massacres and plundering by the Ottomans, their Kurdish collaborators, and others against the "minorities," and even against established American interests, were too similar not to have been implemented by the highest governing authority.

Voluminous state department testimony and other works published in the 1890s describe the Hamidian massacres of the 1890s, which anticipated the larger-scale massacres by the Ottomans and the Committee for Union and Progress (the Young Turks) that began in 1915 and continued into 1923.[6]

At the close of 1895, Alexander W. Terrell, the United States minister to the Ottoman Empire (at Constantinople), sent an urgent message to Richard Olney of the state department about a typical incident.[7]

> No. 722.
> Legation of the United States, *Constantinople, December 15, 1895*. (Received Dec. 31.)
> Sir: I have the honor to inclose herewith the copy of a letter just received from Rev. Dr. C. F. Gates [a representative of the ABCFM and the U.S. state department] dated the 25th ultimo, at Harpoot, with a copy of a sketch of the missionary property which was destroyed in that city.
> The fact that Dr. Barnum [the ABCFM representative] is charged with having instigated the Armenians to revolt shows the extreme danger to which Americans are exposed. The inclosed letter will place your Department in possession of all facts needed to form a correct judgement regarding the burning at Harpoot.
> The mysterious secrecy which here conceals the designs against Christians until the hour when they are to be executed and

the massacres in the six [Armenian] provinces before the Harpoot affair, induced me to telegraph at once, not only to Harpoot but to other interior posts, as to whether our people could reach the seacoast.

A. W. Terrell[8]

The above-mentioned letter from Gates to Terrell reports on the plundering of the missionary properties as follows:

> To us it seems clear that we are confronting a deliberately planned scheme to render the [Turkish] reforms [specified by the Treaty of Berlin] useless by destroying the Christian population. All who are left in the villages are considered Moslems and will be claimed as such by the Government. Moreover no guaranty or pledge is considered sacred. Our lives are safe only so long as the Government considers it expedient to preserve them. . . . The Government did not protect us. . . . No guards were placed at the gates of our premises. Our houses were plundered and burned and we were fired upon under the eyes of the [Turkish] soldiers, who were posted on a hill behind our premises. . . . We were not guarded until after the catastrophe, and then they tried to get us out of the college building in order that they might burn it. . . . They carried kerosene oil, which they poured upon the woodwork and then set fire to it.[9]

Although the ABCFM had been firmly established in Turkey for more than seventy-five years, the missionaries, trained to provide humanitarian assistance, were not adequately prepared for the events that unfolded during and after the 1890s. Often working under the most difficult of circumstances, the members of the ABCFM did, however, promote Armenian awareness and set the stage for an even greater humanitarian movement.

It was in 1895 and 1896 that Clara Barton, the much-revered international champion of humanitarian relief, was summoned into service in Armenia by the ABCFM in Constantinople on an urgent "call for the relief of the terrible sufferings of Armenia, which were engaging the attention of the civilized world."[10]

In reacting to the massacres of the 1890s, foreign missionaries, writers, and political philosophers developed their own discourse about Armenia. Their writings provided the rationale for the massive relief measures implemented during and after World War I, as well as the conviction among enlightened persons that Armenian independence would be the only lasting solution.

For example, British journalist E. A. Brayley Hodgets (a writer for the *London Daily Graphic*), after traveling from Constantinople through Anatolia and into the Caucasus in 1895, wrote this account in *Round about Armenia:*

The theory I had evolved was . . . simple. It was that history was repeating itself, and that we were on the eve of the enfranchisement of Armenia. The dissolution of the Turkish Empire has been going on piecemeal for the last century or so by provinces. Each province falls away from Turkey . . . on the following lines. First, there is a revolutionary movement, then there are massacres, which enlist the sympathy of Europe. These are succeeded by an organized rebellion. . . . Emancipators are usually rather careless about spilling the blood of the people they wish to emancipate. One historical axiom it is well to bear in mind—whenever Turkey is about to lose a province she first massacres the population.

One thing seems to be certain, the [European] Powers appear to have made up their minds that the lives of a few thousand Armenians, more or less, are not worth incurring the risk of a European war. But this is not the first time that the Powers have tried to prevent a war over the Eastern question; nevertheless, they have not been invariably successful.

Therefore, let every humane person, every patriotic Englishman, demand loudly the liberation of Armenia, and never think of the consequences. If we have to face a war let us face it, and remember the cause of the . . . down-trodden is the cause of the British Empire.[11]

The early 1900s became the era of popular epithets about the Armenians. Writers of that period called the merchants and traders of Anatolia the "Christian people of ancient Eden,"[12] "a noble race,"[13] the "first people to embrace Christianity,"[14] whose "origin is lost in the mists of antiquity,"[15] the "guides to the Crusaders,"[16] and "subject to persecution for centuries under Moslem rule."[17] The writers compared them to their own nationalities, regarding them as a downtrodden people under the yoke of Ottoman tyranny.[18] The single most-remembered statement about them was popularized by William Gladstone, the British prime minister, who declared in a speech before Parliament that "to serve Armenia is to serve civilization."

The twentieth century brought more industry, more goods and services, increased social and political awareness, and the realization of a smaller, more interdependent world. The so-called "Armenian question" was part of the Eastern question, which referred to the fate of the Balkans, Anatolia, and the Arab Middle East in light of the decline of the Ottoman Empire. These countries could not readily be freed from Turkish domination. Armenia's case made clear the need for their emancipation. Those who remembered the troubles afflicting her in the 1890s saw how the earlier atrocities grew into full-scale "extermination" or "destruction of a race" in 1915. Meanwhile, the ACASR/NER campaign was popularizing the phrase "remember the starving Armenians." By late 1915, Armenia and Armenians had become household words in America.

The people who had kept Armenian awareness alive from the late nineteenth century included Julia Ward Howe, Alice Stone Blackwell, William Lloyd Garrison, Harriet Beecher Stowe, William Jennings Bryan, Theodore

Roosevelt, Alfred E. Smith, Clara Barton, Susan B. Anthony, Elizabeth Cady Stanton, Arnold Toynbee, and Lord James Bryce.[19] They helped define the Armenian condition in the context of Woodrow Wilson's first presidential administration, with its broadened international awareness.

Chapter Two
Woodrow Wilson's Plan for Armenia

In 1912, in the aftermath of the Italo-Turkish War of 1911 and 1912 that demonstrated Ottoman military weakness, the Balkan Wars erupted and led to the almost total elimination of Ottoman rule over the Balkans and a revival of United States concerns about the Near East. The Armenian question emerged once again from the now-distant memory of the Treaty of San Stefano and the resultant Congress of Berlin, which capped the Russo-Turkish War of 1877 and 1878. This time, however, Western thinkers across the Atlantic embraced the concept of Armenian independence. On the eve of the Second Balkan War, Harry V. Osborne of the American Board of Commissioners for Foreign Missions (ABCFM) advised President Wilson as follows:

> And now, after six centuries of barbaric despotism, the ruling house of Ottoman is crumbling . . . as the inherent forces of the country rise again in violence to assert their existence. Europe is in upheaval. The "balance" of the Great Powers is in danger of breaking under the strain of the Balkan War. The fear of rupture in the world peace is universal. Apparently the thorny case of the Near East has never lost its acuteness.
>
> While Turkey may continue to be a home of contention between the guardians of the peace of the world, who are playing diplomacy against each other and pushing along their own methods of modern civilization to their individual advantage, some problems are already slipping out of Turkish mis-government, that have given rise to so many dangerous complications. The Near East cannot stand to be governed by a rotten system any longer. The moral and intellectual perceptions of the Turk are perverse and stationary. That is where Europe and Asia face each other. . . . [T]hat has been the synopsis of the events in the Near East. . . . Today the lightning is struck in the Balkans. The interests of the powers are more complicated there, and all dread the crisis lest the fuse may explode the bomb of an all-European war. . . . Tomorrow the logical turn is for Armenia; also perhaps, for Syria and possibly for Mesopotamia, and finally to complete the anatomy of the Ottoman Empire, [and] for the heart of the Near East, Asia Minor. And for the good of all concerned, an autonomous Armenia is the best alternative that can enter into the account of a final settlement of the Eastern Question. . . . What have not the Armenians suffered already in the hands of the Turks . . . for their fatherland and for the name of Christianity? . . . Whatever little wealth is left of the wreck of [the] economic resources of Turkish misrule, not only in Armenia, but through many other parts of the empire, is largely due to Armenian thrift and enterprise. . . . The situation might be simplified if an autonomous Armenia was to serve the purpose of conducting her state responsibilities in the

settlement of the Near East. She could then help best manage the interests of the powers in Turkey to general satisfaction. She could be the best medium to bring about a mutual understanding between the Balkan states and the rest of the Near East, from which they are inseparable. . . . The Armenian is the bearer of the torch of civilization in . . . Turkey. . . . Were it not for his subdued humiliation by the Turk, he could have long fulfilled his mission of bringing western thought and methods in the east. An autonomous Armenia would immensely facilitate what is eventually to come.[20]

Osborne also warned of the dangers of delay in creating an autonomous Armenia for the Armenians and presciently noted that "the drift of beaten Mussulmans from the Balkans increases a new source of calamity that imperils Armenia."[21]

George Koolakian, a young Armenian man who had lived in the United States since 1905, realized that the continued intermittent massacres of the Armenian people and the outbreak of the Balkan Wars were destined to impede immigration from Turkey to the United States. He tried repeatedly to secure exit visas from the American consulate in Constantinople for various relatives who remained in the Ottoman Empire during this period. In April 1913, William Wheelock Peet, who maintained ties to the United States diplomatic delegation, responded to Koolakian from his quarters at the ABCFM in Constantinople (see fig. 1 on page 30).

Perhaps the single most defining fact to emerge from the Armenian condition was not the periodic massacre and later genocide of her people in Anatolia, which was of inestimable consequence, but rather the public reaction—the outcry—to the atrocities voiced openly as never before both during and after World War I. Looking back on that era, former president Herbert Hoover made the following observation:

> Probably Armenia was known to the American school child in 1919 only a little less than England. The association of Mount Ararat and Noah, the staunch Christians who were massacred periodically by the Mohammedan Turks, and the Sunday School collections over fifty years for alleviating their miseries—all cumulate to impress the name Armenia on the front of the American mind.[22]

Although important information about Armenia and her people had been recorded from the days of the Egyptian, Babylonian, Assyrian, Persian, Greek, and Roman empires, and considerably later from the thirteenth-century expeditions of Marco Polo, too little consideration had been devoted to assessing Armenia's rightful place among the early contributors of modern civilization until the twentieth century, when much of her destiny was in the hands of the Ottoman Empire. However, the ABCFM, the massacres, the relief effort, the war, and the Allied military presence all played a part in bringing new information about the peoples of the Near East, especially the Armenians, into the cultural awareness of the Western world.

Appalled by what he knew of the Turkish-inflicted atrocities, in 1915, Ambassador Henry Morgenthau sent an urgent appeal to the secretary of state. Responding in record time, Woodrow Wilson's colleagues formed the American Committee for Armenian and Syrian Relief (ACASR). In one of the earliest public statements made by that organization, the cornerstone of their eventual worldwide appeal in the Near East was established (see figs. 2a, 2b, 2c, and 2d on pages 31, 32, 33, and 34).

From 1915 through the end of World War I, the ACASR (which became Near East Relief in 1919) posed a new question as part of their concerted humanitarian campaign.[23] They asked simply, "Who are the Armenians?" That question was asked and answered in a brochure that was distributed by the tens of thousands in cities and towns across the United States in the first massive humanitarian effort of its kind in American history (see figs. 3a, 3b, and 3c on pages 35, 36, and 37).

Many contemporaries believed that Armenia had been in the way of Turkey's expansion, and if the Turkish Empire could not acquire her historical territory by the more subtle process of occupation and amalgamation of the land's inhabitants, she would simply destroy them and have unobstructed pan-Turkish access from the Mediterranean to the Caspian Sea.

Although America was reluctant to become involved in the European conflict, the ACASR program signaled her sense of moral responsibility toward the innocent victims of the war and the massive social upheavals in the Ottoman Empire. Less than a year after the ACASR's charter committee implemented its first effort, the Congress acknowledged the plight of the Armenian and Syrian peoples, thus creating the first legislation to champion a minority cause—an important though little-recognized breakthrough in America's attitude toward minorities everywhere. Signing that legislation into law on 31 August 1916, Woodrow Wilson, in part, addressed the nation with these words:

> And whereas, I feel confident that the people of the United States will be moved to aid these peoples stricken by war, famine and disease;
>
> Now, therefore, I, Woodrow Wilson, President of the United States, in compliance with the said suggestion of the Senate, and the said request of the Congress thereof; do appoint and proclaim Saturday, October 21, and Sunday, October 22, 1916, as joint days upon which the people of the United States may make such contribution as they feel disposed for the aid of the stricken Syrian and Armenian peoples.
>
> Contributions may be addressed to the American Red Cross, Washington, D.C., which will care for their proper distribution.
>
> In witness whereof, I have hereunto set my hand and caused the seal of the United States to be affixed.
>
> Done at the City of Washington this thirty-first day of August, in the year of our Lord one thousand nine hundred and sixteen,

and the Independence of the United States the one hundred and forty-first.[24]

From then on, Western interests began to view Armenian independence as imminent and necessary to securing lasting peace in the Near East and in Europe. On 24 January 1917, Lord James Bryce, by then a seasoned scholar on Armenian affairs, and chairman of the British War Relief Commission in the Near East, wrote to his friend Colonel Edward M. House, a trusted advisor to President Wilson:

> Dear Colonel House:
>
> As you might not otherwise see it, I enclose the most temper-ate editorial which I have seen in our press on the President's most impressive speech in the Senate.[25]
> We warmly appreciate its spirit, and we should like to see the attainment of the conditions which he lays down as preconditions to a League of Peace, and as necessary to ensure stability, content-ment and good will in this distracted Europe. . . .
> Is there any chance that Germany would yield up Lorraine, and Austria the Trentino, and the Turks Armenia? If there is I wish we knew of it. Yet without these concessions, could there be stability and security in Europe?
> I am,
> Sincerely yours,
> James Bryce[26]

Within a year, Mr. Wilson and his closest advisors would begin drafting the articles of his proposed Fourteen Points, the peace program in which they would assert that the non-Turkish nationalities of the Ottoman Empire then under Turkish rule (including, implicitly, the Armenians), "should be assured an undoubted security of life and an absolutely unmoletested opportunity of autonomous development" (Point Twelve), as an integral part of the anticipated peace process in Europe.

Woodrow Wilson cared deeply about Armenia in particular, as evidenced by the following excerpts from two September 1919 talks:

> Then there was another thing we wanted to do, my fellow citizens. . . . We wanted to see that helpless peoples were no-where in the world put at the mercy of unscrupulous enemies and masters. . . . There was a Christian people, helpless, at the mercy of a Turkish government which thought it in the service of God to destroy them. And at this moment . . . it is an open question whether the Armenian people will not, while we sit here and de-bate, be absolutely destroyed. When I think of words piled upon words, of debate following debate, when these unspeakable things that cannot be handled until the debate is over are happening, in

these pitiful parts of the world, I wonder why men do not wake up to the moral responsibility of what they are doing. Great peoples are driven out upon a desert, where there is no food and can be none, and they are driven to die, and then men, women, and children, thrown into a common grave, so imperfectly covered up that here and there is a pitiful arm stretched out to heaven, and there is no pity in the world. When shall we wake up to the moral responsibility of this great occasion?[27]

I believe that there is no region in the world towards which the sympathies of the United States have gone out so abundantly as to the poor people of Armenia, those people infinitely terrified, infinitely persecuted. We have poured out money to relieve their distress. And at every turn we have known that every dollar we spent upon them might be rendered useless by cruel authority over them. Then, under pretense of not being able to control its own affairs in those parts of the empire, the Turkish government might say that it was unable to restrain the horrible massacres which have made that country a graveyard. . . .

Very well [that] Armenia is one of the regions that is to be under trust of the League of Nations. Armenia is to be redeemed. The Turk is to be forbidden to exercise his authority there. And Christian people are not only allowed to aid Armenia but they are to be allowed to control Armenia. So that at last this great people, struggling through night after night of terror, knowing not when they would see their land stained with blood, are now given a promise of safety, a promise of justice, a possibility that they may come out into a time when they can enjoy their rights as free people that they never dreamed they would be able to exercise.

What great humane impulses of the human heart are expressed in this treaty! And we would be recreant to every humane obligation if we did not lend our whole force, if necessary make our utmost sacrifice to maintain its provisions.[28]

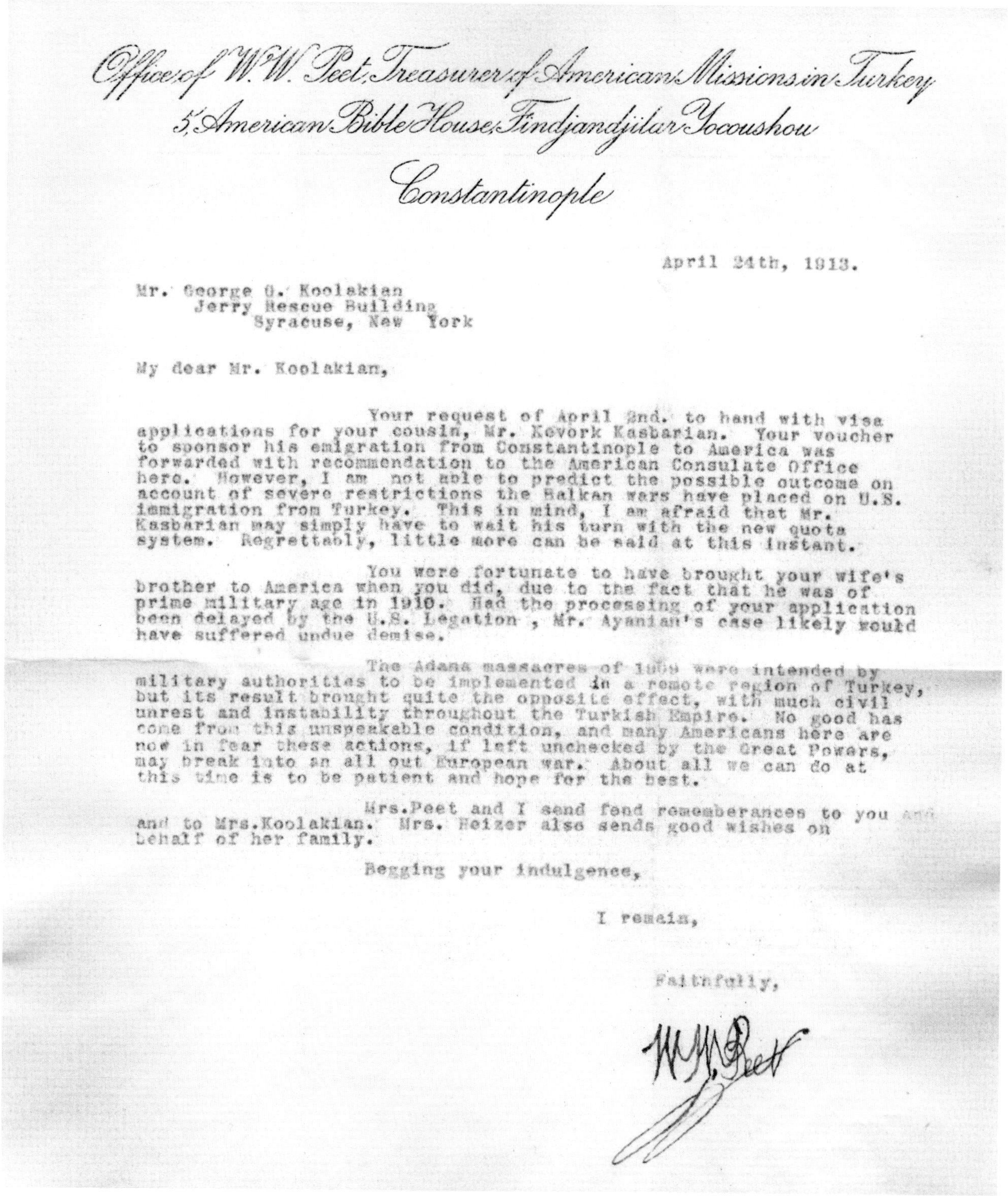

Office of W.W. Peet, Treasurer of American Missions in Turkey

5, American Bible House, Findjandjilar Yocoushou

Constantinople

April 24th, 1913.

Mr. George G. Koolakian
    Jerry Rescue Building
      Syracuse, New York

My dear Mr. Koolakian,

      Your request of April 2nd. to hand with visa
applications for your cousin, Mr. Kevork Kasbarian. Your voucher
to sponsor his emigration from Constantinople to America was
forwarded with recommendation to the American Consulate Office
here. However, I am not able to predict the possible outcome on
account of severe restrictions the Balkan wars have placed on U.S.
immigration from Turkey. This in mind, I am afraid that Mr.
Kasbarian may simply have to wait his turn with the new quota
system. Regrettably, little more can be said at this instant.

      You were fortunate to have brought your wife's
brother to America when you did, due to the fact that he was of
prime military age in 1910. Had the processing of your application
been delayed by the U.S. Legation , Mr. Ayanian's case likely would
have suffered undue demise.

      The Adana massacres of 1909 were intended by
military authorities to be implemented in a remote region of Turkey,
but its result brought quite the opposite effect, with much civil
unrest and instability throughout the Turkish Empire. No good has
come from this unspeakable condition, and many Americans here are
now in fear these actions, if left unchecked by the Great Powers,
may break into an all out European war. About all we can do at
this time is to be patient and hope for the best.

      Mrs.Peet and I send fond rememberances to you and
and to Mrs.Koolakian. Mrs. Heizer also sends good wishes on
behalf of her family.

      Begging your indulgence,

        I remain,

          Faithfully,

Fig. 1. Letter from William Wheelock Peet to George Koolakian, 24 April 1913.

ARMENIA

"A Christian Nation"

HER HEART-RENDING CRY

> We have it on reliable authority that in the last eight months 800.000 Armenian Christians have been massacreed. This is Turkey's long awaited chance. England and France stopped these butcheries in 1860 and 1895 but are now too busy to interfere. Can America do Nothing?

Issued by the Syracuse Fund a Committee for
RELIEF IN ARMENIA

Fig. 2a. Broadside entitled *Armenia, "A Christian Nation": Her Heart-Rending Cry* published in 1915. This was the first official notice distributed by the central New York branch of the American Committee for Armenian and Syrian Relief.

CONTRIBUTIONS

In Cash should be made to

1st National Bank or Syracuse Trust Co.

In Food or Clothing to

552 South Salina Street

A Receiving Station open daily 2 to 5 P. M.

WILL YOU HELP?

By a Cash Contribution or Food or Clothing.

By organizing a Committee in your section of the city to procure aid.

By assisting the Church Committee of your Church.

EXECUTIVE COMMITTEE

BISHOP CHARLES FISKE, D. D.,   CHANCELLOR JAMES R. DAY,

REV. DR. JAMES EMPRINGHAM,   A. W. HEDDEN, M. D.
                        Chairman. REV. J. APPLEBEE,

L. R. C. WHITTAKER,
            Vice-Chairman.   REV. S. H. HALLEDJIAN,

                           MRS. DONALD DEY,

H. P. PHILIBOSIAN,
            Treasurer.   MRS. G. L. BARNARD,

REV. DR. A. C. FULTON,   MRS. H. B. AZADIAN.

ALMUS OLVER,   -   -   -   Executive Secretary,
Headquarters, Y. M. C. A. Building.

Fig. 2b. The appeal flyer that accompanied the broadside entitled *Armenia, "A Christian Nation": Her Heart-Rending Cry* published in 1915.

The Story of a God-Fearing People

(From an address by James Empringham, S. T. D.)

As a plague of locusts sweeps over the face of tthe earth devouring all vegetation, leaving death and desolation behind, so the scourge of Mohammedanism blasted the East in the sixth and following centuries. Christians were murdered by millions and their churches turned into mosques.

Mohammed, the man who was destined to thus butcher and exterminate whole nations of Christians, was born in the year 570 of poor and ignorant parents. At twenty-five Mohammed entered the service of a rich widow as a mule driver. He married this widow the following year, thus acquiring wealth and leisure, which he employed in meditation in the mountains. One day Mohammed returned to his home, saying the angel Gabriel had appeared to him and commanded him to proclaim the unity of God. Mohammed's relatives and friends professed to believe that he had received a revelation from heaven to overthrow Christianity and all other religions. The rapidity with which this Moslem religion exterminated the faith of the Gospel from many lands seems incredible and can be attributed to two causes—sensuality and the sword. Mohammed had nine wives and promised his followers a heaven of sensuality.

Persecuted at first, the little band of Moslems took the sword in self-defense. Ever victorious, the crescent moon, resembling the curved swords of that period, became the symbol of this new religion. The faith of Islam has ever been a religion of blood, for to all followers of the false prophet the slaughter of those who decline to accept the Koran is a religious duty most pleasing to God, and all Moslems who reject the teaching of the Koran and accept any other faith must be put to death. Nothing is more astonishing in history than the wholesale manner in which Christian nations in the seventh century abolished the faith of the Gospel and accepted the new and degrading religion.

Everywhere in the East to-day the traveller sees venerable churches which for ages have done duty as mosques. The most wonderful church I have ever seen is Santa Sophia, Constantinople, built A. D. 552 by the Christian emperor Justinian, and embellished with precious stones from the ancient pagan shrines. But the Moslems in 1453 burst in upon the helpless worshippers in this church, butchering all but the women, who were reserved for a sadder fate. In this as in hundreds of other churches to-day, the cross has been replaced by the crescent, and the Moslem priest preaches each Friday, always holding a drawn sword in his hand, symbolizing the manner in which their faith must conquer the earth.

But one Christian nation—the Armenian—though surrounded and dominated by the Moslems, has ever refused to be bribed or butchered into the false faith. Tradition says that Armenia was converted by the apostles, Bartholomew and Thaddeus. Gregory, the Illuminator, converted the King of Armenia in 285, and it thus became the first national church. The ecclesiastical position of the Armenia church resembles that of the Church of England in that it is national, autonomous and refuses to recog-

Fig. 2c. The first page of *The Story of a God-Fearing People* by James Empringham, a summary of the Armenian people's adherence to Christianity. This narrative accompanied the broadside entitled *Armenia, "A Christian Nation": Her Heart-Rending Cry* published in 1915.

nize the primacy of Rome or Constantinople. In organization also it is akin, as it has always retained the historical episcopate. It acknowledges the Nicene creed as its confession of faith and recognizes the authority of the first three General Councils. The Bible is an open book with it and Bible study and general education have always been encouraged by the church. The Armenian Church had its Syriate version of the scriptures a thousand years before Wycliffe gave the English the Bible in their own language.

Many and merciless have been the Mohammedan attempts to sever with the sword the tie that binds these people to their ancient church. From the seventh to the tenth centuries millions of the Armenian Christians were massacred. Many such slaughters have occurred within the memory of the men still living, one of the most dreadful outbursts being in 1860, when the sword was turned against all Christians in the Turkish empire. At that time France sent an army into Syria and put an end to the massacres. Most of us remember the Armenian massacres of 1895 and 1896. Then the united action of the English clergy so aroused that nation that the British government sent her fleet to say the slaughter must end. England did not merely send a polite note, she sent her battleships and the butchery stopped, for the Sultan knew the British meant business.

We have it on reliable authority that in the last eight months 800,000 helpless Armenian Christians have been put to death. This is Turkey's long awaited chance. England and France are too busy to interfere. Mr. Morgenthau, our ambassador to Turkey, has lodged our protest with the Sublime Porte and the only results seem to have been that nine prominent Armenians were hanged in the streets of Constantinople on the charge of complaining to America. Thus does the infamous Turk show his contempt for this country.

As an example of Turkish persecution Lord Bryce of England, formerly Ambassador to the United States, cites an occurrence which occurred at Trebizond City where the Armenians numbered 10,000. Turkish troops hunted these people, drove them to the shore, took them out to sea, threw them overboard and drowned them all —men, women and children.

From first hand information we know of numbers of men who, seeing their companions pole-axed like cattle, begged for death by shooting, but this plea was denied.

Our National Armenian Committee says:—"Owing to the close censorship of the press, the world is only now learning the facts from eye witnesses and from official documents. It is now unquestionably established that the plan includes the extinction of all the Armenians and probably of other Christian races throughout all of Turkey. The highest Turkish official at Constantinople declares to representatives of foreign governments that this is their purpose, and the local officials in the provinces openly proclaim that such are their peremptory orders from the capital."

Immediate and generous help is necessary to save scores of thousands of lives where utter destitution reigns in the face of an approaching winter. He who gives speedily gives twice.

Armenia needs our help. It needs the help of our government to influence Turkey to cease this frightful work, and it needs the generosity of private individuals to its starving and wretched people.

Fig. 2d. The second page of *The Story of a God-Fearing People* by James Empringham, a summary of the Armenian people's adherence to Christianity. This narrative accompanied the broadside entitled *Armenia, "A Christian Nation": Her Heart-Rending Cry* published in 1915.

AMERICAN COMMITTEE FOR ARMENIAN AND SYRIAN RELIEF

70 FIFTH AVENUE, NEW YORK

INCLUDING WORK OF THE ARMENIAN RELIEF, THE PERSIAN
WAR RELIEF, AND THE SYRIAN-PALESTINE RELIEF COMMITTEES

JAMES L. BARTON, Chairman   SAMUEL T. DUTTON, Secretary   CHARLES R. CRANE, Treasurer

ARTHUR J. BROWN	NORMAN HAPGOOD	JOHN MOFFAT	ISAAC N. SELIGMAN
EDWIN M. BULKLEY	MAURICE H. HARRIS	JOHN R. MOTT	WILLIAM SLOANE
JOHN B. CALVERT	WILLIAM I. HAVEN	FRANK MASON NORTH	EDWARD LINCOLN SMITH
JOHN D. CRIMMINS	HAMILTON HOLT	HARRY V. OSBORN	JAMES M. SPEERS
CLEVELAND H. DODGE	ARTHUR CURTIS JAMES	RT. REV. P. RHINELANDER	OSCAR S. STRAUS
CHARLES W. ELIOT	FREDERICK LYNCH	KARL DAVIS ROBINSON	STANLEY WHITE
WILLIAM T. ELLIS	CHAS. S. MacFARLAND	WILLIAM W. ROCKWELL	TALCOTT WILLIAMS
JAMES CARDINAL GIBBONS	H. PEREIRA MENDES	GEORGE T. SCOTT	STEPHEN S. WISE
RT. REV. DAVID H. GREER			

TO THE FRIENDS OF HUMANITY

Above the din of war and amid its distress and suffering a cry of anguish and appeal is heard in Asia Minor which compels the attention of all civilized peoples. The attempt is made to destroy an ancient people: a people whose citizenship has been the most valuable factor in the Turkish Empire; a people whose love of education and whose ability shown in the fields of commerce and industry have made them most efficient members of the communities in which they reside.

In the heat and madness of war the command was issued to tear these people from their homes and to drive them like herds of cattle to those waste and barren regions where there is little chance of their being able to survive. This is not all. As a part of this process of extermination the able, healthy men, especially the young men and boys, have been separated from their families and either forced to enter the army or have been put to death. The women, without regard to age or state of health, with the children were forced to leave behind nearly all their belongings and to undertake journeys lasting weeks, or even months, with scanty clothing and food, often being the prey of bands of irregular soldiers and criminals.

This process of wiping out an entire people is more cruel and abhorrent than any massacre which modern history records. The American Committee does not undertake to fix the blame but feels sure that those who are guilty will sooner or later have to answer at the bar of public opinion. It is assumed, however, that many people in the Turkish Empire have already protested and view with horror this reversion to extreme barbarism.

The Committee is advised that several hundred thousand Armenians, many of whom have fled to Russia and Persia, are now suffering for food, clothing and shelter. The need is urgent and your aid is solicited.

The American people have responded generously to many calls of mercy during the past year and will not lend deaf ears to this appeal for funds made by Ambassador Morgenthau who in this, as in all other difficult situations, has shown admirable courage and judgment.

Will you, by your gifts, enable our Treasurer to send larger and larger sums in order that the remnant of the Armenian people may be fed, clothed, and if possible reestablished in their homes?

- -

I hereby agree to send to the Treasurer of the American Committee on Armenian Atrocities,

Charles R. Crane, 70 Fifth Avenue, New York, ... *Dollars*

in aid of the suffering Armenians.

(SIGNED) ....

Address ....

Fig. 3a. The appeal letter accompanying the relief campaign brochure entitled *To the Friends of Humanity* published in 1916. This brochure outlines the reasons for the establishment of President Wilson's American Committee for Armenian and Syrian Relief program late in 1915. This type of literature was widely distributed throughout at least twenty-five major cities in which Armenian and Syrian relief offices were first established in the United States.

AMERICAN COMMITTEE FOR ARMENIAN AND SYRIAN RELIEF

70 FIFTH AVENUE, NEW YORK

INCLUDING WORK OF THE ARMENIAN RELIEF, THE PERSIAN WAR RELIEF
AND THE SYRIAN-PALESTINE RELIEF COMMITTEES

JAMES L. BARTON, CHAIRMAN   SAMUEL T. DUTTON, SECRETARY
WALTER H. MALLORY, FIELD SECRETARY   CHARLES R. CRANE, TREASURER

The Committee is composed of some fifty eminent American citizens, wholly non-sectarian, and organized to receive and distribute funds for the purposes of its formation.

The following statements are based upon official documents, dispatches and reports from unquestioned authoritative sources and are made upon a most conservative basis.

THE ATROCITIES

Talaat Bey boasted that he would make the Armenians pray for massacre, and he has.

Of the two million Armenians in Turkey one year ago, at least one million have been killed, driven from the country, forced into Islam, have perished on the way to exile or been deported to northern Arabia.

The Armenians in the army were first brutally put to death; then followed those who had purchased exemption and nearly all able-bodied males above twelve years of age. After this the remaining men, women and children were sent out upon a journey of months, mostly on foot, to the arid regions of Syria and northern Arabia.

These helpless, hopeless refugees were forced out from their homes with little preparation for the journey and with no shelter from the storms or protection from the cold or heat.

A man following one of these caravans for twenty-five miles reported to a United States Consul that he counted over 500 dead bodies on the road.

Women giving birth to children upon the road were forbidden to delay by the way and often died from hemorrhage as they struggled on.

Children by the hundred were cast into rivers by their parents to save them from mortal suffering.

A United States Consul reported that he saw refugees brained with clubs because they, when starving, crowded their guards for food.

Armenian professors in American colleges, with university degrees from European and American universities, were tortured by pulling out their hair and beard and their finger nails, by hanging them up by the arms for hours, and by beating. They were afterwards killed.

Comely women and girls have been in great numbers forcibly taken into Mohammedan harems. Entire towns have been driven to accept Islam to save themselves from death.

The Turkish Government permits no Armenian to leave the country and the closest watch is kept that none escape.

NUMBERS IN DIRE NEED

The United States Consul at Aleppo reports over 150,000 exiles in his district alone, and that is only one of the regions to which these victims are deported. From one-half to two-thirds of those sent from their homes into exile perish on the road.

There are now not less than 600,000 suffering, starving, dying Armenians scattered throughout Turkey and in exile in dire need of immediate help. The United States Consul at Tiflis, Russia, reports 180,000 refugees, many of them in terrible distress, in the four Russian Provinces bordering upon Turkey.

Nearly, if not quite half as many, are in a similar condition in Persia. Over 4,000 have escaped to Egypt and are being cared for there.

Fig. 3b. The first and second pages of the relief campaign brochure entitled *To the Friends of Humanity* published in 1916.

Distress is increasing as the winter comes on and the food supplies of individuals and families are exhausted.

WHO ARE THE ARMENIANS?

The Armenians are from one of the oldest and most notable of ancient races. They were the allies of Cyrus the Great and as a nation figured conspicuously in the history of the country in which they now suffer. Before the attack upon them, there were more than 1,100,000 Armenians in Russia and Persia, to whom are now added nearly, if not quite, 300,000 refugees.

There are probably 660,000 still surviving in Turkey, with more than 100,000 in the United States, Europe, Egypt, and other countries.

They were the first nation to adopt Christianity as their national religion, and to this they have ever adhered.

Armenians have, in all history, won distinction in many departments of human activity and stand second to no Asiatic race, and have shown themselves able successfully to compete in intellectual and commercial pursuits with Europeans and Americans.

Their habits and tastes are domestic, without military ambitions, eager for modern education, industrious and frugal, and preeminently lovers of peace.

This is the people now staggering under the unprovoked blow of heartless assassins and calling mightily to the civilized world for necessary and immediate assistance to save the remnant of the race.

The Armenians in the United States have given over $400,000 for the relief of their stricken people in Turkey.

RELIEF MEASURES

The American Committee is caring for the refugees in Egypt. They have also an American commission in Russia with headquarters at Tiflis working in conjunction with the British Relief Committee under Lord Bryce.

They are providing funds for the relief of the destitute in Turkey through Ambassador Morgenthau and a committee with headquarters in Constantinople.

A constant stream of relief is necessary to save the race. Foodstuffs are plenty in the country which can be purchased for their use. Clothing also can be procured there.

The Committee is endeavoring to secure through our State Department permission to send a relief expedition into the country to search out the sufferers and minister to their need. When this privilege is secured a vastly larger sum will be needed to return the refugees to their homes and reestablish them there upon a self-supporting basis.

The Committee can cable money in any desired amounts to Cairo, Constantinople and Tiflis.

The expenses of the central offices in New York are paid by members of the Committee as a special gift.

One dollar now will be worth five in the spring. The need is immediate and imperative.

Ambassador Morgenthau, the United States Consuls, and the missionaries and teachers in the American schools plead for means to furnish relief to the multitudes whose pitiful condition cries out mightily for aid.

AUXILIARY RELIEF COMMITTEES

It is important that at every considerable center of population an auxiliary relief committee be formed to keep local interest alive and to raise funds to be sent through the Central Committee. It is imperative that one Central Committee shall direct remittances, that they be equitably and judiciously divided.

Remittances should be sent, in bank draft, money order, or registered letter, to Charles R. Crane, Treasurer, 70 Fifth Avenue, New York, N. Y.

Fig. 3c. The third and fourth pages of the relief campaign brochure entitled *To the Friends of Humanity* published in 1916.

MISSIONS IN TURKEY OF THE AMERICAN BOARD

OFFICE OF TREASURER

W. W. PEET. LL.D. TREASURER
L. R. FOWLE, ASSISTANT TREASURER

استانبول ــ آمريقان خان

TELEGRAPHIC ADDRESS
PEET - STAMBOUL.

بيت ــ استانبول

AMERICAN BIBLE HOUSE
STAMBOUL-CONSTANTINOPLE

September 21, 1918

Mr. George G. Koolakian
Jerry Rescue Building
Syracuse, N.Y.

My dear Mr. Koolakian:-

your kind letter of August 12th, addressed
to me in care of the American Consulate here was forwarded to
hand in due course, and I thank you for it.

In regard to Mardiros and Mariam Ayanian,
who wish to emigrate to America, I am not able to say with any
certainty when their case will be brought before the Commission.
I regret it may have to wait consideration, with so many others,
until after the war. The matter is now so closely regulated by
the Consulate that is impossible for me to suggest anything else.
I have referred your appeal with letter to the Commission, asking
every consideration for the Ayanians with special regard to your
sponsorship.

We are informed by State Department author-
ity that this horrible war is is expected to end soon and, accord-
ingly, I am requested by the American Committee to return to the
States to address the issue of Armenian independence. I intend
to do this forthwith, considering all of the facts. After all
that has happened, this matter is not to be taken lightly. I
recommend that you and Mr. Azadian maintain your connections with
Mr. Cleveland H. Dodge at our offices, One Madison Avenue, New
York, for he will, no doubt, advise you as to our meeting and
long-range objectives. I have already taken this up with him, so
he will expect to hear from you. Kindly inform Mr. Azadian also.

Please remember me to Mrs. Koolakian and
to your son, the latter who impressed me as a bright young boy so
many years ago when they left Constantinople for America.

With good assurances to your family and
all friends, I am,

Faithfully yours,

Fig. 4. Letter from William Wheelock Peet to George Koolakian, 21 September
1918.

CHAPTER THREE
THE RISE OF THE ARMENIAN INDEPENDENCE MOVEMENT

With the end of World War I and the drafting of the League of Nations covenant all but complete, the Armenian independence movement in the United States emerged from obscurity. Although it was not yet formally recognized, the earliest reference to the "American Committee" is contained in a memorandum drafted by Dr. James L. Barton, Cleveland H. Dodge, and William Wheelock Peet in mid-November and forwarded to Secretary of State Robert Lansing for Woodrow Wilson's consideration.[29] On 22 November, Lansing transmitted that memorandum along with a summary of its contents to the president.[30] By the end of 1918, a loosely structured yet formal organization had evolved under the title of the American Committee for the Independence of Armenia (ACIA).

Initially composed of some seventy-five prominent Americans who supported Armenia's democratic liberation, this organization was to engage an even wider circle of top-level American and world figures from among the Allied Nations. From the beginning of the ACASR/NER, it was understood that America had a moral obligation to assist Armenia. Woodrow Wilson's concept of "peace through justice" came to express itself in the Armenian independence movement.

Few students of public affairs understand how the Armenian independence movement was conceived in the United States. Nor do they know of the individuals who first brought the idea of Armenian independence to bear so profoundly upon the social and political institutions of America. The movement's origins were American, arising out of the urgent call for Armenian and Syrian relief. However, its history was soon obscured in the aftermath of the state department's almost abrupt withdrawal from participation in the ACIA during 1920 and 1921.

To trace that history, one need only look back to the summer of 1918 when the end of the "Great War" was already being anticipated in the administrative halls of Washington, D.C. George Koolakian learned of American plans for Armenian independence perhaps unexpectedly. On 12 August 1918, he wrote to his friend William Wheelock Peet via the United States legation in the Ottoman Empire to inquire about the immigration status of family members for whom he had previously filed American visa applications in Constantinople.[31] On 21 September 1918, Koolakian received Peet's reply (see fig. 4 on page 38).

This letter marked the beginning of Koolakian's unplanned association with the Armenian independence movement during the next several months. Work was already underway between the ABCFM and the ACASR/NER on the one hand, and the state department on the other, in planning the ACIA.

Based on the story of central New York's involvement in the movement, one might suppose that the U.S. government was motivated by domestic politics to help Armenia during the early 1900s. On the contrary, American politicians had little, if anything, to gain internally by helping Armenia's cause, since the Armenians represented a small fraction of America's overall voting population. Other factors came to light as Woodrow Wilson promoted his democratic peace program.

Although Wilson began his second term of office as "the man who kept us out of war," that tenuous platform was about to crumble as the United States was irrevocably drawn into the European conflict. America did not want to become involved in the war, but was drawn into it, and its participation in the war in Europe only strengthened Wilson's resolve to seek justice for the Armenian people.

Central New York played an important part in the American-inspired Armenian independence movement of the early 1900s. Some of its citizens nurtured remarkable, although mostly confidential, connections with the most powerful national and international circles of the period.

CHAPTER FOUR
THE AZADIANS, THE KOOLAKIANS, AND THE MISSIONARIES

Abdul Hamid II's ascension to the Ottoman throne began the reign of the so-called "bloody sultan" (1876–1909). It was marked by mounting political and social instability and by intermittent atrocities perpetrated on the minority peoples living within the empire, especially the Armenians and the Greeks. Strife and corruption at the highest levels of the political infrastructure became the pretext for the "sick man of Europe" to affix the blame for the ills of Turkish misrule upon the Armenians, who in reality had been among the most socially and economically productive elements within the Ottoman Empire. It was "Turkey's long awaited chance," culminating in the bloodiest period (1915–23) of Turkish rule.[32]

The 1878 treaty resulting from the Congress of Berlin required that the Ottomans respect the civil rights of all non-Turkish citizens. The minorities were not generally regarded as citizens; they were the "subjects" of the sultan of Turkey, according to the United States state department records. Flouting the treaty, the Ottomans carried out massacres and deportations, thinking they would not be noticed by the Western world. The opposite effect was due to the increasing Western presence in Turkey, notably the influx of missionaries from the ABCFM and consular officials from the United States and Europe. Until the mid-1890s, key urban coastal areas of Anatolia were little affected. The Hamidian program of Armenian extermination was carried out through periodic massacres in the interior at Van, Hadjin, Kars, Moush, Sivas, Aintab, and Marash, among others.

Around 1880, the ABCFM had drawn its own map of the Ottoman Empire, dividing it into ten administrative "fields," or districts, each having its own American schools, hospitals, and orphanages, all attended by the ABCFM administrators and staff.[33] From the 1880s on, a young, well-educated administrator, William W. Peet, was appointed by the ABCFM in Boston to oversee their foreign operations within the Ottoman Empire. Becoming administrative treasurer, Peet was soon stationed at the ABCFM headquarters in Constantinople. Because of the Hamidian massacres and the rise of the Young Turk movement, Peet presided over the most difficult period ever experienced in the administrative history of the ABCFM—anywhere. It was through Peet's offices in Constantinople that all of the funding from America was distributed to the administrative districts. At the same time, he became the recipient of detailed condition reports from each of these areas.

Most, if not all, of those reports were eventually forwarded to the Boston office via the American and British consular mails and were therefore free of Ottoman censorship. In this way, William Peet maintained his vital connection to the international headquarters of the ABCFM, and to Julia Ward Howe, Clara Barton, Alice Stone Blackwell, Edwin Bliss, William Lloyd Garrison and his family, the Beecher family, and other influential Americans who supported the organization.

Later correspondence from Peet indicates that he and his family were grateful for the assistance of the Azadian family. Well educated and Westernized, the

Azadians were able to introduce the Peets to the Ottoman world and to help them adapt to a new lifestyle in the Ottoman Empire. The Peet family visited frequently, and their son "Willie" later acknowledged that he grew up in the 1890s in Constantinople feeling that the Azadians were like his own family.[34]

Because of his international association with the American and British consulates in Constantinople and his connection with Julia Ward Howe and Alice Stone Blackwell, William Peet was to be of inestimable help to young Harutun Azadian and, later, to George Koolakian. Following one of the smaller-scale Hamidian massacres in Smyrna (1895) in which Akabi Kechebashian (Azadian's future wife), her family, and her friend Johanna Zimmer were unexpectedly involved, William Peet arranged to send the two women to Germany on special assignment to relocate a group of Armenian orphan girls for the ABCFM (see fig. 5 on page 45).[35] Peet later facilitated the Azadians' passage to America with Zimmer in 1899. Through Julia Ward Howe and Alice Stone Blackwell, Peet also arranged passage to America for two members of the Koolakian family at the request of Harutun and Akabi Azadian.[36]

Born in the Ottoman Empire in 1875 and 1876, respectively, Azadian and Koolakian traced their ancestral roots in the Marmora district of Constantinople from Byzantine times, prior to the Ottoman conquest of 1453. Both had been raised in families that embraced their ancient Christian tradition, though in that cosmopolitan community, they were exposed to French, German, and Turkish, as well as much earlier Armenian, Greek, and Jewish Sephardic influences.

The Azadians for generations had been engravers and designers for the Ottoman sultans (see fig. 6 on page 46). They worked for F. Loeffler and Company, the official French-based Ottoman government printing house in Constantinople.[37] They also traded with many commercial, educational, and religious establishments throughout the region and nurtured business contacts in eastern and western Europe. Earlier in the 1820s and 1830s, the Azadians had established business relationships with the ABCFM. Harutun Azadian's grandfather Artemy (Harutun) Azadian designed stationery and business cards for the ABCFM main offices.[38] He also produced school diplomas, commencement cards, and programs for recitals and concerts for the various American schools and colleges throughout the ABCFM districts of the Ottoman Empire.[39] By the 1850s, the Azadian name was known as far away as the United States.

The Azadians were also known for their support of Florence Nightingale (1820–1910), the English nurse and hospital reformer. In 1854, the British secretary of war dispatched her to the Crimean War front. Stationed in Constantinople with a battery of English-trained nurses, she established efficient nursing departments at the British military hospital, which was within walking distance of the Azadian summer home. When Nightingale appealed to local citizens and missionaries for support, the Azadians responded.

Nicolai Artjemeff Artenjen (Negale Ardemitz Azadoff, in Russian), a paternal uncle of young Harutun, helped to maintain a family commission to the Russian Imperial Court in St. Petersburg that had lasted for almost two hundred years (see fig. 7 on page 47). Both branches of the Azadian family were members of a cosmopolitan, propertied upper class whose business travels extended into eastern and western Europe, as well as the Crimea (see fig. 8 on page 48).[40]

Their homes, Romanova-Arjuttinoff (winter residence), along the northern shore of the Bosphorus at Rumeli Hissar, and Anadoli-Arjuttinoff (summer home), along the northeast Marmora shore in Constantinople, were well known to visiting officials and missionaries from the ABCFM (see fig. 9 on page 49). The Constantinople Azadians also maintained a private retreat at Chermoog, the famous warm mineral springs health resort near Bursa, south of the central Marmora district.[41] Chermoog was an important meeting place for traveling members of the ABCFM, especially during the winter months. Harutun Azadian met many ABCFM representatives when he was a child in the 1870s and 1880s, long before he departed for America.

As a result of his connection with the ABCFM, Azadian met his future bride, Akabi Kechebashian, a well-educated young Armenian woman who came to work for the ABCFM as a music teacher at their American Bible House. Akabi was a member of a prominent family from Caesarea (or Kayseri) and Smyrna, who had received her education at the American Girls School in Kayseri and was later sent by her family to study music in Vienna.[42] Successfully completing her program, Akabi assumed her teaching position at the American School for Girls in Constantinople. Following the 1895 Armenian massacres in Smyrna, she completed additional study at the Leipzig Conservatory, under ABCFM sponsorship.[43]

Soon after taking her teaching assignment, Akabi Kechebashian befriended an older member of her teaching staff, Johanna Zimmer (see fig. 10 on page 50), a German missionary who had taught for the ABCFM since 1890, after completing her education at Rockford Seminary in the United States.[44] Zimmer took her first teaching assignment at the ABCFM's American Bible House in Constantinople in 1890 and 1891. Thoroughly dedicated to the missionary cause, she maintained an interest in Armenian affairs for the remainder of her life, long after coming to the United States with the Azadian, Kechebashian, and Zimmer families in 1899.

Zimmer had familial connections with Otto von Bismarck, the German chancellor.[45] That family connection made it possible for her and Akabi to go to Germany in 1896 and to America in 1899 at the behest of the ABCFM. Twenty-four-year-old Harutun Azadian accompanied them, having plans to study advanced mechanical engineering at the Stuttgart Polytechnicum (see fig. 11 on page 50).[46]

In February 1897, while completing his higher technical education in Germany, Azadian met through the Zimmer family the well-known electrical scientist Charles Proteus Steinmetz, who was visiting on assignment from America. Through Steinmetz, Azadian was introduced to many coworkers of Thomas Edison, who would later organize themselves as the Edison Pioneers.[47] This business connection would become important to him when he moved to the United States. Azadian and Steinmetz remained friends until the latter's death in 1923 (see figs. 12a, 12b, and 13 on pages 51 and 52).

The Koolakian family had resided in the southern Marmora district of Constantinople for hundreds of years. Surviving records suggest the prominent standing of the Koolakian clan. Their trade symbols—the five-pointed star (which adorned their buildings) with its matching Persian teardrop O (for the number five)—appear in documents from medieval times. The Koolakians had garnered enough respect and influence to induce the Ottoman treasury to issue legal coinage bearing their symbols from the late eighteenth century to the early 1900s (see fig. 14 on page 53).

In his youth, George Koolakian had apprenticed in custom clothing design and merchant tailoring, becoming thoroughly accomplished in the art (see fig. 15 on page 54). Bringing that reputation to America after the turn of the century, he built a considerable clientele, and his company was often called the "Cadillac" of custom clothiers in central New York. His wife, Elizabeth Ayanian, whom he betrothed in 1902, came from a family of well-to-do plantation and vineyard owners with extensive properties in the southern Marmora district. Her father, Mardiros Ayanian, was a securities investor and moneylender with investments in Credit Foncier Égyptien, a French international banking house that helped finance the Suez Canal.

The elder Ayanians had grown up with the Armenian Protestant movement of the 1830s and 1840s at Banderma, a picturesque seaport city in the southern Marmora district.[48] Supporters of the ABCFM, they had educated their two children at local ABCFM-sponsored American schools. Elizabeth received her later secondary and higher education at the American Girls School at Adapazar on the Anatolian mainland southeast of Constantinople.

From the day of their meeting in America in 1905, Harutun Azadian and George Koolakian forged a "khunami," a family relationship that was to last for the remainder of their lives; they soon became partners in family and civic affairs.[49] Although they had no knowledge of one another before coming to the United States, they shared an ethnic Armenian background as former "subjects" of the Ottoman sultan from the Marmora district of Constantinople and strong connections with the ABCFM. That background had a great deal to do with their eventual involvement in the American Committee for the Independence of Armenia.

When Azadian and Koolakian came to America, they found themselves in a hospitable central New York community.

Lifte der aufgenommenen Kinder in Bebek.

Asnif.   Angine.   Takuhi Michaelian.
    Adrine.   Sirpui.   Heropsime.   Satenik.   Prapion.   Armenuhi.   Lusinia.
Osanna.   Armenuhi Tschamjan.   Isabelle.   Kunik.   Elmonia.   Gräfin Groeben.   Perus.   Wartanusch.   Satenik.   Jertschanik.
Jsgubi.   Osanna.   Elpis.   Siranusch.   Imastik.   Seraphian.   Heropsime.   Syneard.   Howard.   Naseni.   Schnorig.   Arasi.
        Schnorig Tschalakjan.   Makruhi.   Dirubi.   Hirantubi.
    Wartubi.   Saruhi.   Takuhi.   Jodoria.   Aravni.   Adrine.   Siranusch Mathiosjan.

Fig. 5. "Armenian Orphans of the Massacres of Smyrna" (in faded handwrit-
ing at the top of the photograph) at the orphanage of the American Board of
Commissioners, Bebek, Constantinople, 1896. Assigned to Johanna Zimmer
and Akabi Kechebashian, these orphan girls were sent by the American Board
to Germany where they were resettled with German families. Completing his
technical education at the Stuttgart Polytechnicum, Harutun Azadian followed Zimmer and Kechebashian in the fall of 1896. This photograph was taken
in Constantinople, carried to Germany, and published in its present form in
Stuttgart. Photograph by Gaillard for the American Board of Commissioners,
1896. Courtesy of the Azadian Collection.

Fig. 6. *Sultans of the Imperial Ottoman Empire, 1300–1789,* a commemorative oil painting commissioned by Selim III for the Azadian family in recognition of their long-standing work for the Ottoman government. The ascension of Sultan Selim Kahn III to the Ottoman throne in 1789 established the French rococo influence within the culture of the Ottoman Empire. With that "new order" came this decree of "historical privilege" given to the Azadoff Artemjeff-Artenjen family in Constantinople. After more than two hundred years, this remarkable work underwent restoration by one of the foremost painting conservators in the field.

НЕ ̆УВѦ́ДАЄМЫЙ ЦВѣ́ТЪ ПРЄСТЫ́Ѧ БЦЬІ.

Fig. 7. Engraving entitled *Madonna and Christ Child Enthroned*. A particularly striking example of A'Zad(ian) family artwork is this meticulously executed engraving by Prokofi Ivanovitsch Artemjeff (1733–1811) during the middle of the eighteenth century for the "Holy Synod," the governing body of the Russian Orthodox Church in St. Petersburg. Here mother and child are crowned at the seat of the church by the archangels Gabriel and Michael. An exemplary engraving, it is typical of the many commissions produced by members of the Azadian family—in this case by "Ivanovitsch Zaduni II" for the Eastern Orthodox Church as well as the Russian Imperial Court during the reign of Catherine the Great and the later Romanovs. Although beautiful and highly prized themselves, these engravings often served as design templates employed by the Artemjeff-Azadian family in their engraving of gold and silver religious devotionals, icons, reliquaries, Bible covers, jewelry, and other forms of official adornment employed in the church and by members of Russia's Romanov dynasty.

CARTE ALBUM

Fig. 8. The Azadoff-Artenjen brothers in 1867. These enterprising brothers in their thirties had entered their father's established business in Constantinople and St. Petersburg. Specialized engravers, lithographers, and jewelers, they executed commissioned work for the Ottoman and Russian courts, and had business connections throughout eastern and central Europe and the Middle East. The eldest of the two brothers, Negale Ardemitz Azadoff Artenjen (Nicolai A. Artenjen) or "Artjemeff" (1832–83) (right), came to administer much of the family enterprise in Russia, eastern Europe, and the Caspian port city of Baku, while Harutun Azadian's father, Mardiros Artin Azadoff Artenjen or "Arjuttinoff" (1837–1901) (left), centered his business activities in Constantinople and western Europe, executing work for the sultan's High Regulatory Commission, as well as for the noted firm of F. Loeffler and Company. Affiliated with the famed Russian-born Armenian painter Hovhannes Aivazian or "Aivazovsky" and his school of art in Constantinople, the Azadian brothers were related to him through their paternal great-grandfather "Hayvaz," the eighteenth-century engraver-technician who had maintained earlier family ties in Constantinople, south Poland, and St. Petersburg, long before the "Aivazians" moved from Constantinople to the Crimean port city of Theodosia in the early 1800s. A marked family resemblance between the Azadian brothers (especially Nicolai) and Hovhannes Aivazovsky is evident in contemporary photographs of this period. Carte Album portrait, Constantinople, 1867. Courtesy of Arshalouis Azadian Randall.

Fig. 9. View of Marmora/Rumeli Hissar/Constantinople by Harutun Bab Azadian, 1884. Azadian was first educated by tutors who came to the family home, where he took classical instruction under Khrimian Hayrik, who would become the celebrated Armenian patriarch of Constantinople. He later attended the Sourp Astvadzadzin Holy Cross School. Following in his father's footsteps, he received formal instruction in calligraphy and engraving at the Mekteb-i-Seneyeh while attending the famous Hovhannes Aivazovsky school of art in Constantinople. He completed a formal apprenticeship in sculpting and engraving in Paris under master artist August le June Rubin in 1894 and 1895. Azadian's ability in detailed art and mechanical work was well advanced at an early age and is evident even in the amateur drawing of a view of Marmora, a scene he captured from Romanova Arjuttinoff, looking towards the Bosphorus-Marmora Sea inlet—remarkably, when the lad was but nine years old. The almost photographic drawing depicts Archbishop Khrimian approaching the Azadian home to administer one of the youth's lessons. Azadian's formal education was completed from 1896 to 1899 when he studied mechanical engineering at the Stuttgart Polytechnicum while serving a related apprenticeship.

Fig. 10. Portrait of Johanna Zimmer (left) and Akabi Kechebashian (right) in 1894. This photograph was taken while the two women were teaching at the American Bible House of the American Board of Commissioners for Foreign Missions in Constantinople. Courtesy of the Zimmer Trust.

Fig. 11. Portrait of Harutun Bab Azadian by Sebah and Joaillier in Constantinople in 1894. This photograph was taken just before Azadian's departure to go to Paris for an apprenticeship in sculpting and engraving. Courtesy of Antaram and Ardemis Desteian.

Fig. 12a. Exterior view of the Lauf Café in Gilf in the Isar River valley in Bavaria, Germany. Harutun B. Azadian met here with Charles P. Steinmetz and his associates from the General Electric Company, who were visiting Europe early in 1897. Records in the Azadian Collection indicate that Azadian met Steinmetz here on at least two occasions. The early 1897 trip must have been a welcomed one for Steinmetz because it marked his first return to Germany, his homeland, since his arrival in the United States almost nine years earlier.

Fig. 12b. Steinmetz group at the Lauf Café, ca. 1898. Seated from left to right are Walter Knight, Albert G. Davis, Edward Bentley, Charles A. Coffin (president of the General Electric Company), and William L. Emmet. Standing from left to right are Hans Zimmer, Max Deri, Edison Pioneers Sigmund Bergmann and Johann Schuckert, Ernst Danielson, Charles Steinmetz, James J. Wood, and Harutun B. Azadian.

Fig. 13. Charles Steinmetz at his home in Schenectady, New York, in 1913. Steinmetz presented this photograph to the Azadian family in 1913 during one of his visits to their Syracuse residence. They had met Steinmetz in Germany in February 1897 through mutual friends Hans and Johanna Zimmer, and remained friends until the scientist's death in 1923. Steinmetz's sympathies toward the Armenians resulted from his long friendship with the Zimmer and Azadian families. He became a supporter of the American Board of Commissioners for Foreign Missions, financially aiding their Armenian orphans program in Constantinople during the early 1900s. His later support of Near East Relief and the Armenian independence movement in America is well documented in the Azadian-Koolakian holdings. Courtesy of Arshalouis Azadian Randall.

Fig. 14. Both sides of a coin bearing the Koulakian (the ancient spelling of Koolakian) trade name and symbols. This Ottoman currency surfaced in New York in an international listing of the Bosco Auction House in 1987. It was sold twice before it was incorporated into the collection of Manuel Panossian, who regards it as a unique find. The trade coin is illustrated here courtesy of Manuel Panossian and Dr. Levon Saryan.

Fig. 15. The Garabed (Charles) Koolakian family in Banderma, a seaport in the southern Marmora district of the Ottoman Empire in 1879. From left to right are Pirapion (Mrs. Garabed), Garabed (Charles), and Kevork (George) Koolakian. Young George Koolakian was born in 1876 into a middle-class family of custom tailors and confectioners. He attended the Armenian Apostolic Church School in his hometown and the École du Dessin in Constantinople, becoming proficient in pattern making, graphic technology, and design. George Koolakian came to America in 1905, bringing his wife and son here in 1908 with the help of the American Board of Commissioners for Foreign Missions. In Syracuse, he established the Custom Garment Making Company, which exists today as Koolakian and Manro Menswear in Hanover Square.

CHAPTER FIVE
ARMENIANS IN SYRACUSE, "CITY OF CHURCHES"

When Azadian and Koolakian first set foot on American soil, few Armenian families had settled in the Syracuse region. A John Bayerian had come to Syracuse in 1893 from the port of Philadelphia to work at the Solvay Process Company, a recent successor to the Syracuse Coarse Salt Works. He had fled the 1890 Armenian massacres at Marash, a town with a significant Armenian population in Cilicia in the Ottoman Empire. In Syracuse, he and his family found accommodating support from Helen and Frances Gifford, members of central New York's prominent Gifford family, wealthy land owners who had maintained a long association with the local Protestant Reformed movement.[50]

Azadian did not go to Syracuse because of any connection with its early Armenian settlers. He went there because of his associations with Johanna Zimmer and the ABCFM.[51] Zimmer's cousin Julia Hineback and Julia's husband, George F. Hine, were also members of Syracuse's Protestant Reformed community. George was an established attorney, and Julia taught German at Syracuse University (see fig. 16 on page 58).

From the pre–Civil War period, central New York had been among the active centers for the Protestant Reformed movement. Syracuse was first distinguished as the "village of churches" and then, after its incorporation in 1848, as the "city of churches," the majority of its early settlers having come from the reformed New England religious tradition. In central New York, that tradition expressed itself in a strong "underground" antislavery movement. After the Civil War and the end of the abolition movement, the older well-to-do crusaders turned their attention to other humanitarian efforts. From the 1870s through the 1890s, they embraced issues of women's suffrage, child labor, education, homelessness, and unemployment. Many local citizens took up the Armenian cause because of their connections with nationally known reformers such as Julia Ward Howe, Harriet Beecher Stowe, William Lloyd Garrison, Alice Stone Blackwell, Clara Barton, William Jennings Bryan, Theodore Roosevelt, Charles Evans Hughes, Alfred E. Smith, Susan B. Anthony, and Elizabeth Cady Stanton—all of them sympathizers of the Armenian cause.

Although its Armenian population was never large enough to distinguish Syracuse as a major Armenian center, the city's religious and humanitarian proclivities attracted displaced Armenians to the area and kept an awareness of their plight alive throughout the region. The Armenian settlers of the 1890s—including the Azadians, Altoonjians, Bayerians, Desteians, Garabedians, Gertmenians, Kechebashians, Philibosians, Rejebians, Seferians, and the Yeranians—came to Syracuse because of their connections with the missionaries of the ABCFM, and the newcomers received assistance from citizens affiliated with the mission movement.

Other Armenian families—such as the Aghaians, Aiqounis, Apikians, Ayanians, Babikians, Danielians, additional Desteians, Enfijians, Haigazians, Hamamjians, Hanessians, Keledjians, Koolakians, Manoogians, Mardians, Minasians, Ozanians, Roomians, Saxenians, Schmavonians, Tufenkjians, Vetzikians, Yessaians, and the Zahrajians—who arrived soon after, came to central New York as a result of existing ties to previously established members of the Armenian community.[52]

One local Armenian, Harry (Harutun) Philibosian, became an important friend and associate of Azadian and Koolakian (see figs. 17 and 18 on pages 59 and 60). He had established himself in Syracuse in 1894 after fleeing the Armenian massacres at Hadjin, a town in Cilician Armenia. Two years later, he brought other members of his family to America. Having an extensive knowledge of the Oriental rug trade, he formed his own business, H. P. Philibosian Persian Palace Rug Company. Like Azadian and Koolakian, Philibosian had missionary connections and became involved in the Armenian relief and independence movements.

All the local Armenians were aided in some way by the strong mission movement in central New York. Among the local citizens who assisted them were Helen, Frances, William H., and (later) Rosamond Gifford; Mr. and Mrs. George F. Hine; Mr. and Mrs. Robert Dey; Donald Dey; George Wagner; Charles Andrews; Mr. and Mrs. E. Stowe Beecher (of nearby Orwell, New York); John C. Birdlebough; Thaddeus C. Sweet (of Phoenix, N.Y.); A. C. Fulton; James Roscoe Day; and Charles Fiske.[53] During their early days in central New York, the Armenians of Syracuse were the grateful beneficiaries of an "open door" policy on the part of these compassionate people (see figs. 19 and 20 on pages 61 and 62).

By the advent of World War I, the almost five hundred Armenians of Syracuse were assimilated community members (see fig. 21 on page 63). They had become shopkeepers, store owners, restauranteurs, factory workers, and salespeople (see figs. 22, 23, and 24 on pages 64, 65, and 66). Many local Armenians labored to bring other displaced family members to the region.[54]

The founding of Syracuse University in 1870 had also been a product of the Protestant Reformed movement. Its founders had close ties with the American Board of Commissioners for Foreign Missions. The institution was established as a Methodist college, and it continued to maintain strong Protestant Reformed connections well into the twentieth century. Under several of its administrators, the university also contributed significantly to the Armenian cause, especially during the lengthy tenure of its fourth chancellor, the Reverend James Roscoe Day (see fig. 25 on page 67), a Methodist minister whose Syracuse University appointment (1894–1922) coincided with the worst atrocities against the Armenians.

Through his connections with the ABCFM and the affiliated Central New York Reformed Protestant Ministers Association, Day became a founding trustee of the ACASR upon its nationwide establishment late in 1915. A social leader and educator, Day spearheaded the local and regional philanthropic effort with James Empringham of the ABCFM (Boston), assisting with the resettlement of displaced Armenians in central New York. Chancellor Day also established a refugee student program at Syracuse University, where many Armenians and Greeks received higher education. This program extended well beyond Day's tenure at Syracuse University, in cooperation with the nationwide Near East Relief program.

Mr. and Mrs. E. S. Beecher exemplified the New England Protestant Reformed movement. Descended from colonial stock, they were longtime evangelicals whose ancestors came from Connecticut and New York City. Their family included Henry Ward Beecher and Harriet Beecher Stowe, bulwarks of the abolitionist movement. There were familial connections as well between the Beechers and Julia Ward Howe, one of the driving forces behind the American Board of Commissioners for Foreign Missions, whose family had supported that organization from its early years (see fig. 26 on page 68). Howe arranged passage to America for George Koolakian's wife and son (see fig. 27 on page 69). It is an interesting fact that, until Syracuse's first Armenian church was founded, many of the region's older Armenian families attended weekend prayer meetings and worship services at the Beecher farm in Orwell, New York (see figs. 28 and 29 on pages 70 and 71). On special occasions, services were administered by visiting missionaries who traveled there under the auspices of the ABCFM.[55]

The Armenian Fourth Presbyterian Mission Church was established in 1912 and the first Armenian Apostolic Church, a year later. George Koolakian, a member of the Presbyterian church's steering committee, became its first president in 1912, with Harry P. Philibosian as treasurer and Hagopos Haigazian as secretary.[56] Harutun Azadian, Sarkis Manoogian, Hagop (Jacob) Yessaian, and Mihran Danielian were also founding associates.[57] Mrs. Azadian organized and directed the church's music program, and Reverend Samuel Halladjian became the first full-time minister of its congregation.[58]

In addition to giving the Armenians an increased sense of permanence, community identity, and cohesiveness, the new churches had another important function. The Armenian Fourth Presbyterian Mission Church in particular maintained a vital connection to the ABCFM (see fig. 30 on page 72).[59] The church also connected local Armenians with the American community at large. A few years later, the church, with its trustees, assumed an active role in establishing the first central New York regional branch of the American Committee for Armenian and Syrian Relief, working in late 1915 with James L. Barton, Robert Chambers, and James Empringham of the ABCFM.[60]

Fig. 16. Julia Hineback Hine, Syracuse, New York, in 1897. A teacher of German
at Syracuse University, Julia Hineback Hine was a member of the local Protestant
Reformed community. She and her husband, George F. Hine, helped Armenian
immigrants such as Akabi and Harutun Azadian settle in Syracuse. Courtesy of
the Julia Hine Trust and Arshalouis Azadian Randall.

Coatsworth,   Syracuse, N. Y.

Fig. 17. Harutun (Harry) Panos Philibosian. After arriving in the United States in 1894, Philibosian founded the H. P. Philibosian Persian Palace Rug Company, at 414 South Salina Street (along Syracuse's main north-south thoroughfare). A successful entrepreneur, he rebuilt a complete city block of downtown Syracuse, establishing a strip of stores and a movie theater prior to World War I. Philibosian belonged to many public-spirited organizations and was a prominent member of the central New York Masonic Order, and he was the sponsor of George Koolakian when he joined this fraternal organization. Philibosian's connection with the American Board of Commissioners for Foreign Missions brought him many important contacts in the United States. He was an active supporter of the Syracuse Symphony Orchestra, a founder of Syracuse's Armenian Fourth Presbyterian Mission Church, and a trustee and treasurer (1915–22) of central New York's American Committee for Armenian and Syrian Relief, which brought Syracuse into Woodrow Wilson's nationwide Armenian relief program. His nephew, the late Stephen Philibosian, whom he brought to America in 1909, apprenticed in Philibosian's Syracuse business and later established Philibosian stores in Auburn, New York; Atlanta, Georgia; and Philadelphia, Pennsylvania. Stephen also established the Stephen Philibosian Foundation, supporting education and relief efforts in the Middle East. The late Charles W. Jacobsen, a noted Oriental rug authority, began his career as an apprentice to H. P. Philibosian at his Syracuse establishment in the early 1920s.

Fig. 18. View of downtown Syracuse in 1906. George Koolakian took this photograph from the entrance to H. P. Philibosian Persian Palace Rug Company at 414 South Salina Street. In those days, most people traversed the city by horse and carriage, although street rail transportation existed on the main thoroughfares, and the Erie Canal still plied the east-west route through the center of downtown as it had for more than eighty years. There were few Armenians in Syracuse then, but there was abundant opportunity. Harutun Azadian, who arrived in 1899, established a gauge factory; by 1916, he employed scores of others in four different company locations throughout central New York. In the photograph's left foreground is William H. Gifford, Esq., former Syracuse district attorney and one of Koolakian's earliest friends and professional associates in central New York. Koolakian, next to the right, stands in front of the streetcar.

Fig. 19. Portrait of Harutun and Akabi Azadian with their firstborn daughter, Arshalouis Johanna Zimmer. This photograph was taken in April 1902, by which time Azadian was an accomplished precision gauge maker and an aspiring patentee. At the time, his first registration was pending with the U.S. Department of Commerce in Washington, D.C., for the first adjustable rack-and-pinion mechanism. He received United States patent 714.771 on 2 December 1902. Courtesy of Emma Azadian Cargen.

Fig. 20. Calling card engraved in 1901 by Harutun Azadian for central New York proprietor George Wagner. For a brief time after coming to America, Azadian engraved such calling cards and commercial broadsides while moonlighting as a precision instrument maker. Courtesy of Arshalouis Azadian Randall.

Fig. 21. Armenians of Syracuse in 1914. A few local Armenians gathered for this photograph during an annual picnic in Onondaga Park. In the 1890s, they had begun to settle in the area. By 1914, the Armenian population was not large, but it was visible because of its involvement with national and international Armenian relief organizations, especially the American Board of Commissioners for Foreign Missions. The highlight of this event was the presence of the ABCFM trustee Alice Stone Blackwell (seated in the center row, fourth from the right) and missionary instructor Johanna Zimmer (the next person to the right). In 1915, the ABCFM established an American Committee for Armenian and Syrian Relief station here. Through that organization, central New York was brought into Woodrow Wilson's national Armenian relief program.

Fig. 22. Portrait of George Koolakian in 1911. This photograph was taken at Koolakian's firm, the Custom Garment Making Company of Syracuse. He designed custom patterns and clothing for such individuals as George Eastman, Walter Hickey (later founder of the Hickey-Freeman Clothing Company), Charles Steinmetz, H. Gosman Wynkoop (War Industries Liberty Loan Committee officer), Elihu Root, Crandall Melvin, E. S. Beecher, William H. and Rosamond Gifford, New York State assembly speaker Thaddeus Sweet, New York appellate judge Charles Andrews, and members of Cazenovia's Lincklaen-Ledyard family. Long before World War I, Koolakian's reputation was that of a master artisan. A modest family man, a gentleman farmer, and an avid reader, he was a member of many public-spirited organizations and a respected brother in the central New York Masonic Order. He was an apolitical person, dedicated to humanitarian causes and ever aware of the new-found freedom afforded to his family in America.

Fig. 23. Custom Garment Making Company, Jerry Rescue Building, Syracuse, New York. This staff photograph was taken in the waiting room of George Koolakian's clothing design establishment. In his youth, Koolakian had apprenticed in custom clothing design and tailoring. Bringing those skills to America after the turn of the century, he built a considerable clientele; his company was often called the "Cadillac" of custom clothiers in central New York. In addition to his many individual patrons, Koolakian was producing custom design work for such clothing makers as Walter Hickey, W. S. Peck, Ingalls and Haskins, Crego and Company, Kent and Miller, and W. B. Schantz, among a host of other northeastern clothing manufacturers who were brought into the Clothing Consortium of the first United States Industrial Advisory Commission (IAC) during the early weeks of World War I. Reorganized into the U.S. War Industries Board and headed by Bernard Baruch during Wilson's second presidential term, the IAC's Industrial Clothing Consortium and the Merchant Tailors and Designers Association of America figured prominently in the greatly increased production of military uniforms for the war. Already well known through these channels, Koolakian was an advisor to Charles G. Volk, chief of the USIAC Military Uniform Design Procurement Division under Lindley M. Garrison, President Wilson's former secretary of war. Interestingly, Garrison himself would join other high-ranking United States government officials in becoming a charter committee member of the American Committee for the Independence of Armenia upon its formation immediately following the armistice of 1918. Most of Koolakian's staff (above) contributed to war production. Standing, from left to right, are Misak DerOhanesian, George G. Koolakian, Stephen Philibosian (the youngest staff member at age twenty), Yegeshea Ayanian, Krikor Apikian, and Apraham Kurdian. Seated, left to right, are Minas Apikian and Emil Rossi.

Fig. 24. View of the Erie Canal in 1906. This downtown view looking west from the Salina Street Bridge shows that Syracuse was still a canal town. Harutun Azadian, a gauge maker and inventor about to change jobs, was employed by the Standard Gauge Manufacturing Company at 107 North Franklin Street (in the background on the right beyond the trees), while moonlighting in his new partnership, the Syracuse Gauge Company, at nearby Pearl and East Willow streets. Already self-employed, George Koolakian was about to establish his store in the top floor of Syracuse's Jerry Rescue Building (in the background on the left) adjacent to the Erie Canal. Charles Steinmetz and associates Ernst Berg and Albert Rohrer (from the General Electric Company, Schenectady, New York), whom Azadian had met in Germany in 1897, frequented Syracuse in 1906. Their mathematical calculations had facilitated the building of the high-tension alternating-current power lines linking Syracuse with the Ontario Power Company generating plant at Niagara Falls beginning in 1906.

Fig. 25. Photograph of Syracuse University Chancellor James Roscoe Day. Through his connections with the American Board of Commissioners for Foreign Missions (ABCFM) and the affiliated Central New York Reformed Protestant Ministers Association, Day became a founding trustee of the regional American Committee for Armenian and Syrian Relief (ACASR) upon its nationwide establishment late in 1915. A social leader and educator, Day spearheaded the local and regional philanthropic effort with James Empringham of the ABCFM (Boston), assisting with the resettlement of displaced Armenians in central New York while establishing a refugee student program at Syracuse University, where many Armenians and Greeks received higher education. This program extended well beyond Chancellor Day's tenure (1894–1922) at Syracuse University in cooperation with the nationwide Near East Relief program. Courtesy of Syracuse University Archives.

Fig. 26. Photograph of Julia Ward Howe (1819–1910). A writer, poet, lyricist, and prominent American reformer, Howe is perhaps best remembered for authoring the "Battle Hymn of the Republic," written during the Civil War. From the early 1840s, she served the American Board of Commissioners for Foreign Missions (ABCFM), and she, more than any other American of her time, brought about needed aid to survivors of the atrocities within the Ottoman Empire. She also helped to focus international attention on the plight of the Armenians. Howe was a founding member of *Armenia*, one of the first Armenian-English journals published in America. (Following her death, this publication was renamed the *Oriental World,* later becoming the journal *New Armenia*.) From the offices of the ABCFM in Constantinople, Howe helped arrange safe passage to America for George Koolakian's wife and son in 1908. Courtesy of Arshalouis Azadian Randall.

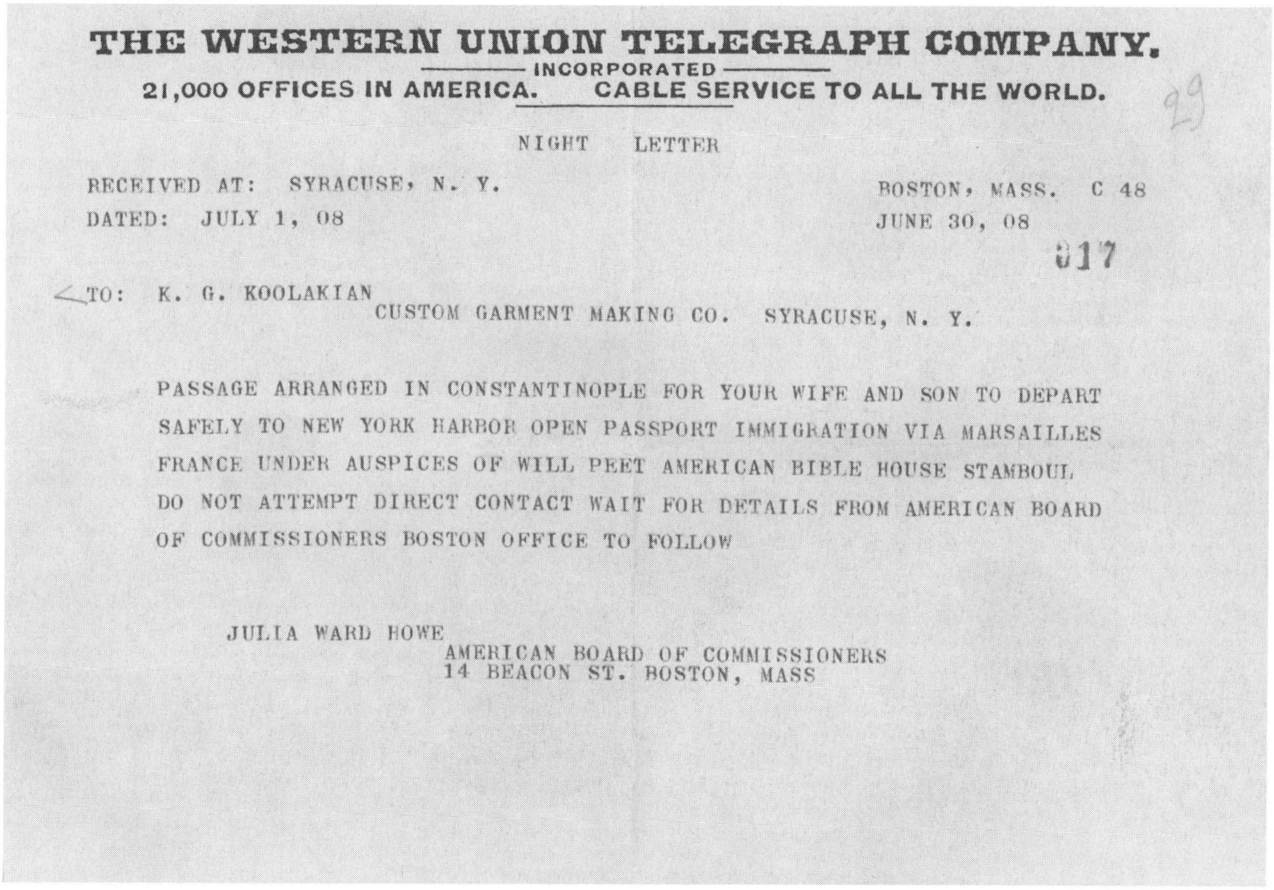

THE WESTERN UNION TELEGRAPH COMPANY.
————— INCORPORATED —————
21,000 OFFICES IN AMERICA.   CABLE SERVICE TO ALL THE WORLD.

NIGHT   LETTER

RECEIVED AT: SYRACUSE, N. Y.   BOSTON, MASS.   C 48

DATED: JULY 1, 08   JUNE 30, 08

TO: K. G. KOOLAKIAN
            CUSTOM GARMENT MAKING CO.   SYRACUSE, N. Y.

PASSAGE ARRANGED IN CONSTANTINOPLE FOR YOUR WIFE AND SON TO DEPART
SAFELY TO NEW YORK HARBOR OPEN PASSPORT IMMIGRATION VIA MARSAILLES
FRANCE UNDER AUSPICES OF WILL PEET AMERICAN BIBLE HOUSE STAMBOUL
DO NOT ATTEMPT DIRECT CONTACT WAIT FOR DETAILS FROM AMERICAN BOARD
OF COMMISSIONERS BOSTON OFFICE TO FOLLOW

            JULIA WARD HOWE
                 AMERICAN BOARD OF COMMISSIONERS
                 14 BEACON ST. BOSTON, MASS

Fig. 27. "Night Letter" from Julia Ward Howe. This document confirms the arrangements for George Koolakian to bring his family to America. In 1905, he had arrived in the United States alone with the help of American friends, but it took him three years to establish himself with sufficient savings to send for his wife and son. Koolakian never forgot what the American Board of Commissioners for Foreign Missions had done for him, and for the rest of his life, he remained committed to their humanitarian activities.

Fig. 28. Beecher Farm, Orwell, New York, in 1910. Until Syracuse's first Armenian church was founded in 1912, many of the region's Armenian families attended weekend prayer meetings and services at the farm of Mr. and Mrs. E. S. Beecher. Longtime supporters of the missions in the Ottoman Empire, the Beechers were members of the well-known Reformed Protestant family that included the abolitionists Henry Ward Beecher and Harriet Beecher Stowe. On this occasion, the three children of Akabi and Harutun Azadian received baptism administered by the Right Reverend Doctor Daniel Hand from the American Board of Commissioners for Foreign Missions. Rev. Hand's family had early connections with Thomas A. Edison, and this extended to collaborative work between Edison, Harvey S. Firestone, Henry Ford, and George Washington Carver. Standing from left to right are Ezekyel Seferian, Eleanor Azadian (child), Mary Kechebashian (sister-in-law of Harutun Azadian), R. Erazian, Akabi Azadian, Harutun Azadian, Mrs. E. S. Beecher, and Mr. E. Stowe Beecher (behind the chair). Seated from left to right are Arshalouis Azadian, Johanna Zimmer (a missionary), Emma Azadian, Mrs. Metaxsis, and the Right Reverend Doctor Daniel Hand (seated in the chair). Photograph by George Koolakian.

Fig. 29. Immigrants from the southern Marmora district of Anatolia pictured at the Beecher Farm in 1906. These were among the first Armenians to settle in Syracuse in the early 1900s. They participated in worship services sponsored by the American Board of Commissioners for Foreign Missions at the E. Stowe Beecher farm in Orwell, New York, and organized informal meetings at their local residences. Their early steering committee led to the formation of the Armenian Fourth Presbyterian Mission Church, Syracuse's first Armenian church, in 1912. The early committee included, standing from left to right, Sarkis Manoogian and Mihran Danielian and, seated from left to right, Hagop (Jacob) Yessaian, George Koolakian, and Hagopos (Jacobus) Haigazian.

Fig. 30. The Armenian Fourth Presbyterian Mission Church founded in 1912. This modest gothic church, located at the intersection of South Salina, Jefferson, and Onondaga streets in Syracuse, was central New York's first Armenian church. It was initially sponsored by the Central New York Presbytery, an affiliate of the American Board of Commissioners for Foreign Missions, and organized by George G. Koolakian, who became its first president in 1912. On 7 September 1915, this church received news of Ambassador Morgenthau's urgent cable alerting the secretary of state of atrocities against Armenians in the Ottoman Empire. The American Board, the central New York Reformed Protestant Ministers Association, and community members met here to plan their response to the crisis. In December 1915, they established one of the first regional branches of the American Committee for Armenian and Syrian Relief in the United States.

CHAPTER SIX
AMBASSADOR MORGENTHAU'S WARNING

In the spring of 1915, renewed and heightened Ottoman atrocities against the Armenians drew worldwide attention. However, concern about the extent of the destruction of the Armenians arose after Ambassador Morgenthau cabled Secretary of State Robert Lansing on 3 September imploring him to take immediate action. Within four days, the ABCFM relayed the content of his cable to members of the Armenian Fourth Presbyterian Mission Church in Syracuse (see fig. 31 on page 75).[61]

Morgenthau's cable had a strong and immediate result in Washington among members of Woodrow Wilson's administration. It prompted Cleveland Dodge, John Mott, Charles Crane, and Stephen Wise to work with the ABCFM to form the ACASR. Lastly, it sent a ripple through urban communities around the country, including Syracuse, New York.[62] Dismayed by the news contained in Morgenthau's cable, on 9 September, George Koolakian addressed a communication (now lost) to President Woodrow Wilson, who responded with a telegram dated 12 September (see fig. 32 on page 76).

In late September, the chairman of the ACASR, James Barton (see fig. 33 on page 77), dispatched his associate Robert Chambers to Syracuse to start a local ACASR relief station there. Syracuse was one of the first of twenty-five urban communities to assume that responsibility.

A news release published in the *Syracuse Post-Standard* on 29 September indicates that a planned mass meeting to be held at the Armenian Fourth Presbyterian Church on Sunday, 3 October, "is in line with the nationwide movement to organize a relief fund" under Robert Chambers (of the ABCFM).[63] The release further states that Dr. Chambers had come to Syracuse to address the Central New York Protestant Ministers Association on the adoption of a resolution to establish a local chapter of the ACASR.

While he was in Syracuse, Chambers met with the local Armenians to enlist their help in planning the new chapter.[64] The mass meeting at the Armenian Fourth Presbyterian Mission Church drew more than two hundred and fifty local Armenians, who spoke out against the massacres. Judge Charles Andrews of the New York Appellate Court and other local prominent Americans addressed the Armenian issue.

By late fall 1915, the first central New York headquarters of the ACASR had been established at Syracuse's Young Men's Christian Association (YMCA) building through an arrangement with John R. Mott, international secretary of the YMCA, and Almus Oliver, the Syracuse representative of the American Board of Commissioners for Foreign Missions. Reverend Dr. James Empringham of the ABCFM was appointed chairman of the local committee. The first public leaflets and broadsides were "[i]ssued by the Syracuse Fund a Committee for Relief in Armenia" under Empringham's direction (see figs. 2a, 2b, 2c, and 2d on pages 31, 32, 33, and 34). (The executive committee is listed on the broadside.) Azadian and Koolakian did not serve on the local committee in an executive capacity. However, they did maintain an active connection with the national headquarters of the ACASR (see fig. 34 on page 78).

In his earliest Syracuse public addresses, Dr. Empringham quoted the most recent news received from Ambassador Morgenthau as follows:

> We have it on reliable authority that in the last eight months 800,000 Armenians have been massacred. This is Turkey's long awaited chance. England and France stopped these butcheries in 1860 and 1895, but are now too busy to interfere. Can America do nothing?[65]

Morgenthau, who became an early trustee of the ACASR's national committee, had further statements:

> Owing to the close censorship of the press, the world is only now learning the facts from eye witnesses and from official documents. It is now unquestionably established that [Turkey's] plan includes the extinction of all Armenians and probably of other Christian races throughout all of Turkey. The highest Turkish official at Constantinople declares to representatives of foreign governments that this is their purpose, and the local officials in the provinces openly proclaim that such are their peremptory orders from the capital.[66]

As a result of Ambassador Morgenthau's extensive work with the ACASR (particularly after resigning his post as ambassador to Turkey), Azadian, Koolakian, and Philibosian met with him on several occasions in New York City as regional liaisons for the Armenian and Syrian Relief effort. Morgenthau, Empringham, and Chambers, working in conjunction with Bishop Charles Fiske of the regional Episcopal diocese, became strong voices in the Syracuse community.[67] It was through such cooperative efforts that the ACASR campaign entitled "Armenia, 'A Christian Nation': Her Heart-Rending Cry" was brought to the central New York area. Documents in the Azadian-Koolakian Papers indicate that the "Syracuse Fund a Committee" was kept well informed of all the ACASR efforts on the national and international levels, bringing assistance to Armenian refugees via the ABCFM in Russia, Syria, Egypt, and throughout the Near East in conjunction with the British Relief Committee under Lord James Bryce, the former British ambassador to the United States.[68]

The national committee of the ACASR was composed of some fifty eminent American citizens. Azadian, Koolakian, and Philibosian would be in regular contact with them during the next five years.

CLASS OF SERVICE	SYMBOL
Day Message
Day Letter	Blue
Night Message	Nite
Night Letter	N L

If none of these three symbols appears after the check (number of words)this is a day message. Otherwise its character is indicated by the symbol appearing after the check.

WESTERN UNION
TELEGRAM
NEWCOMB CARLTON, PRESIDENT

CLASS OF SERVICE	SYMBOL
Day Message
Day Letter	Blue
Night Message	Nite
Night Letter	N L

If none of these three symbols appears after the check (number of words)this is a day message. Otherwise its character is indicated by the symbol appearing after the check.

```
1MA QRU   115 NL NL
            BOSTON MASS SEPT 7 1915 2 PM

K G KOOLAKIAN PRES ARMENIAN PRESBYTERIAN MISSION SYRACUSE NY
  H HAIGAZIAN SECTY
                                          094

NOTIFY CONTENT OF AMBASSADOR MORGENTHAU CABLE AS FOLLOWS

TO SECRETARY OF STATE WASHINGTON 1005 SEPT 3 1915 9 AM MINISTER OF WAR
HAS PROMISED TO PERMIT DEPARTURE OF SUCH ARMENIANS TO THE UNITED STATES
WHOSE EMIGRATION I VOUCH AS BONA FIDE DESTRUCTION OF ARMENIAN RACE IN
TURKEY IS PROGRESSING RAPIDLY MASSACRE REPORTED AT ANGORA AND BROUSSA
WILL YOU SUGGEST TO CLEVELAND DODGE CHARLES CRANE JOHN R MOTT STEPHEN
WISE AND OTHERS TO FORM COMMITTEE TO RAISE FUNDS AND PROVIDE MEANS TO
SAVE SOME OF THE ARMENIANS AND ASSIST THE POORER ONES TO EMIGRATE AND
PERHAPS ENLIST CALIFORNIA OREGON AND WASHINGTON TO TRANSPORT SOME OF
THESE PEOPLE DIRECT TO THEIR SHORES VIA PANAMA CANAL
      MORGENTHAU AMERICAN AMBASSADOR CONSTANTINOPLE

R CHAMBERS
      AMERICAN BOARD OF COMMISSIONERS

                            RECD SYRACUSE NY SEPT 8 1915
                                            10 AM
```

Fig. 31. Telegram from the ABCFM officer Robert Chambers to George Koolakian, 7 September 1915. Four days after Ambassador Henry Morgenthau Sr. informed the state department of systematic massacres of Armenians in the Ottoman Empire, the American Board of Commissioners for Foreign Missions conveyed Morgenthau's message to Syracuse liaisons at the Armenian Fourth Presbyterian Mission Church.

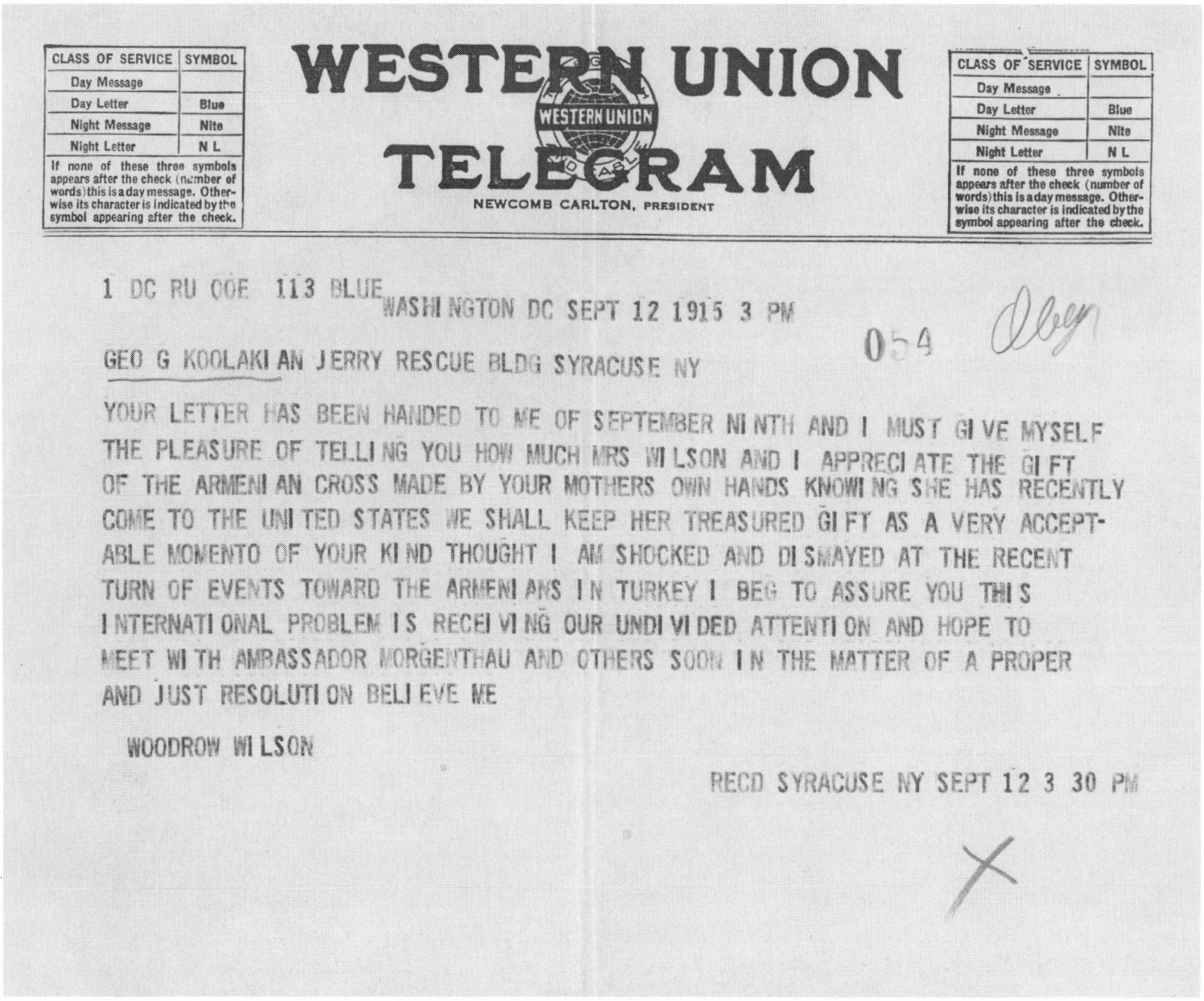

CLASS OF SERVICE	SYMBOL
Day Message	
Day Letter	Blue
Night Message	Nite
Night Letter	N L

If none of these three symbols appears after the check (number of words) this is a day message. Otherwise its character is indicated by the symbol appearing after the check.

WESTERN UNION
TELEGRAM
NEWCOMB CARLTON, PRESIDENT

CLASS OF SERVICE	SYMBOL
Day Message	
Day Letter	Blue
Night Message	Nite
Night Letter	N L

If none of these three symbols appears after the check (number of words) this is a day message. Otherwise its character is indicated by the symbol appearing after the check.

1 DC RU OOE 113 BLUE WASHINGTON DC SEPT 12 1915 3 PM

054

GEO G KOOLAKIAN JERRY RESCUE BLDG SYRACUSE NY

YOUR LETTER HAS BEEN HANDED TO ME OF SEPTEMBER NINTH AND I MUST GIVE MYSELF
THE PLEASURE OF TELLING YOU HOW MUCH MRS WILSON AND I APPRECIATE THE GIFT
OF THE ARMENIAN CROSS MADE BY YOUR MOTHERS OWN HANDS KNOWING SHE HAS RECENTLY
COME TO THE UNITED STATES WE SHALL KEEP HER TREASURED GIFT AS A VERY ACCEPT-
ABLE MOMENTO OF YOUR KIND THOUGHT I AM SHOCKED AND DISMAYED AT THE RECENT
TURN OF EVENTS TOWARD THE ARMENIANS IN TURKEY I BEG TO ASSURE YOU THIS
INTERNATIONAL PROBLEM IS RECEIVING OUR UNDIVIDED ATTENTION AND HOPE TO
MEET WITH AMBASSADOR MORGENTHAU AND OTHERS SOON IN THE MATTER OF A PROPER
AND JUST RESOLUTION BELIEVE ME

    WOODROW WILSON

RECD SYRACUSE NY SEPT 12 3 30 PM

Fig. 32. Telegram from Woodrow Wilson to George Koolakian, 12 September 1915.

Fig. 33. Post–Civil War portrait of Dr. James L. Barton. This photograph was taken while Barton was serving as an executive officer of the American Board of Commissioners for Foreign Missions in Boston and a trustee of Robert College in Constantinople. His work exemplified the humanitarian and intellectual objectives of the ABCFM. He authored numerous authoritative works and guided the board's operations in many ways. In 1915, he joined the American Committee for Armenian and Syrian Relief, working with Cleveland H. Dodge, Samuel Dutton, John Mott, and Stephen S. Wise, who elected him chairman of that body. Barton's committee advised President Wilson of the need to establish support for an Armenian independence movement in the United States as a prelude to the adoption of his Fourteen Points and the League of Nations covenant. The resultant organization, the American Committee for the Independence of Armenia, was established in New York in December 1918. Both Barton and Chambers had known the Azadian family in Constantinople. Courtesy of Arshalouis Azadian Randall.

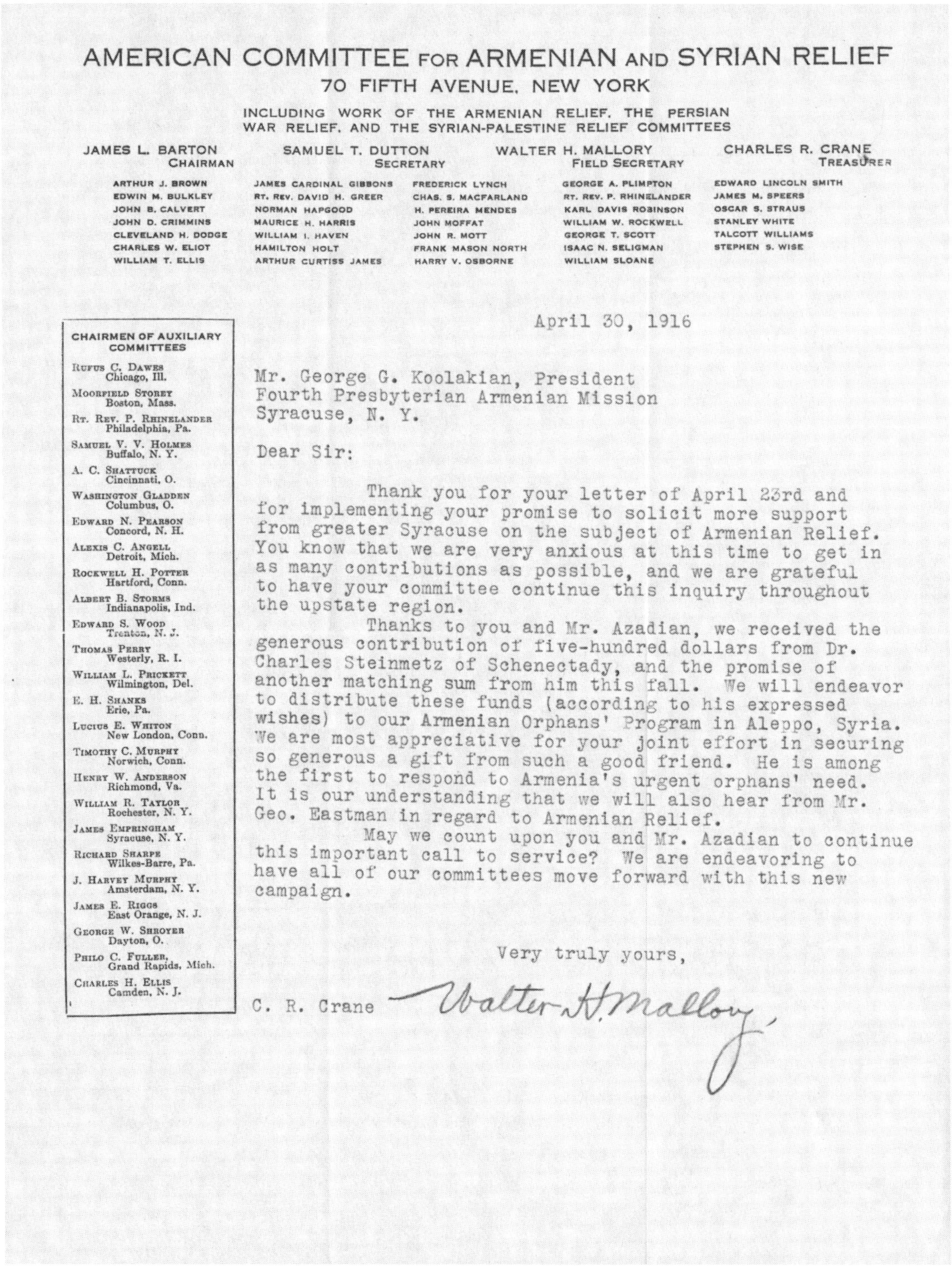

AMERICAN COMMITTEE FOR ARMENIAN AND SYRIAN RELIEF
70 FIFTH AVENUE, NEW YORK
INCLUDING WORK OF THE ARMENIAN RELIEF, THE PERSIAN WAR RELIEF, AND THE SYRIAN-PALESTINE RELIEF COMMITTEES

JAMES L. BARTON, Chairman; SAMUEL T. DUTTON, Secretary; WALTER H. MALLORY, Field Secretary; CHARLES R. CRANE, Treasurer

ARTHUR J. BROWN
EDWIN M. BULKLEY
JOHN B. CALVERT
JOHN D. CRIMMINS
CLEVELAND H. DODGE
CHARLES W. ELIOT
WILLIAM T. ELLIS
JAMES CARDINAL GIBBONS
RT. REV. DAVID H. GREER
NORMAN HAPGOOD
MAURICE H. HARRIS
WILLIAM I. HAVEN
HAMILTON HOLT
ARTHUR CURTISS JAMES
FREDERICK LYNCH
CHAS. S. MACFARLAND
H. PEREIRA MENDES
JOHN MOFFAT
JOHN R. MOTT
FRANK MASON NORTH
HARRY V. OSBORNE
GEORGE A. PLIMPTON
RT. REV. P. RHINELANDER
KARL DAVIS ROBINSON
WILLIAM W. ROCKWELL
GEORGE T. SCOTT
ISAAC N. SELIGMAN
WILLIAM SLOANE
EDWARD LINCOLN SMITH
JAMES M. SPEERS
OSCAR S. STRAUS
STANLEY WHITE
TALCOTT WILLIAMS
STEPHEN S. WISE

CHAIRMEN OF AUXILIARY COMMITTEES
Rufus C. Dawes, Chicago, Ill.
Moorfield Storey, Boston, Mass.
Rt. Rev. P. Rhinelander, Philadelphia, Pa.
Samuel V. V. Holmes, Buffalo, N. Y.
A. C. Shattuck, Cincinnati, O.
Washington Gladden, Columbus, O.
Edward N. Pearson, Concord, N. H.
Alexis C. Angell, Detroit, Mich.
Rockwell H. Potter, Hartford, Conn.
Albert B. Storms, Indianapolis, Ind.
Edward S. Wood, Trenton, N. J.
Thomas Perry, Westerly, R. I.
William L. Prickett, Wilmington, Del.
E. H. Shanks, Erie, Pa.
Lucius E. Whiton, New London, Conn.
Timothy C. Murphy, Norwich, Conn.
Henry W. Anderson, Richmond, Va.
William R. Taylor, Rochester, N. Y.
James Empringham, Syracuse, N. Y.
Richard Sharpe, Wilkes-Barre, Pa.
J. Harvey Murphy, Amsterdam, N. Y.
James E. Riggs, East Orange, N. J.
George W. Shroyer, Dayton, O.
Philo C. Fuller, Grand Rapids, Mich.
Charles H. Ellis, Camden, N. J.

April 30, 1916

Mr. George G. Koolakian, President
Fourth Presbyterian Armenian Mission
Syracuse, N. Y.

Dear Sir:

Thank you for your letter of April 23rd and for implementing your promise to solicit more support from greater Syracuse on the subject of Armenian Relief. You know that we are very anxious at this time to get in as many contributions as possible, and we are grateful to have your committee continue this inquiry throughout the upstate region.

Thanks to you and Mr. Azadian, we received the generous contribution of five-hundred dollars from Dr. Charles Steinmetz of Schenectady, and the promise of another matching sum from him this fall. We will endeavor to distribute these funds (according to his expressed wishes) to our Armenian Orphans' Program in Aleppo, Syria. We are most appreciative for your joint effort in securing so generous a gift from such a good friend. He is among the first to respond to Armenia's urgent orphans' need. It is our understanding that we will also hear from Mr. Geo. Eastman in regard to Armenian Relief.

May we count upon you and Mr. Azadian to continue this important call to service? We are endeavoring to have all of our committees move forward with this new campaign.

Very truly yours,

C. R. Crane — Walter H. Mallory

Fig. 34. Letter from Walter H. Mallory to George Koolakian, 30 April 1916. Mallory was the first field secretary for the ACASR/NER and also the fund-raising coordinator for the organization.

CHAPTER SEVEN
ARMENIAN-SYRIAN RELIEF DAYS

Azadian and Koolakian remained involved with the national American Committee for Armenian and Syrian Relief throughout 1916, especially during President Wilson's Armenian-Syrian Relief Days, observed on 21 and 22 October throughout the United States by proclamation of Congress (see the appendices on pages 129, 130, 131, and 132).[69] The program was promoted through churches in urban centers across the country (see fig. 35 on page 82). Local newspapers published stories about the Turkish massacres and the efforts of the ACASR. A letter dated 21 October 1916 from Charles V. Vickrey, secretary of the ACASR, notified all regional coworkers of the act of Congress and presidential proclamation of the Armenian-Syrian Relief Days of 21 and 22 October 1916 (see fig. 36 on page 83). Koolakian and Philibosian attended the regional and national meetings held in New York City to launch the Armenian-Syrian Relief Days program, and they did so as representatives of Syracuse's Armenian Fourth Presbyterian Mission Church and the newly established Syracuse branch of the ACASR. John W. Lieb, an officer with the Association of Edison Illuminating Companies and an early executive member of the ACASR, acknowledged their attendance in a letter (see fig. 37 on page 84).

In 1916, George Koolakian learned from the ACASR's Foreign Office about the unexpected demise of his sister and other family members (see fig. 38 on page 85). A year and a half later, the *Syracuse Post-Standard* featured a story about the salvation of the Roomian family, distant relatives of Koolakian's wife, Elizabeth (Ayanian) (see fig. 39 on page 86). In March of 1918, after residing in Syracuse for five years, Peter H. Roomian received long-awaited news from his family, which had endured much suffering at the hands of the Turkish gendarmes along their two-thousand-mile deportation on foot from Constantinople to Palestine. The letter had been delayed two months in reaching Roomian.

Through various civic affiliations, Azadian, Koolakian, and Philibosian were able to generate additional participation in the local ACASR campaign. The three friends were members of the central New York Masonic Order, the Liberty Loan Committee, the YMCA, the Syracuse Businessmen's Association (predecessor to the Syracuse Chamber of Commerce), and the Rotary Club (see figs. 40 and 41 on pages 87 and 88).

During that early campaign in Syracuse, the Reverend "Billy" Sunday (William Ashley Sunday) held evangelistic meetings. A one-time well-known major league baseball player of the 1880s and 1890s, Sunday had been increasingly influenced by the Protestant Reformed movement, eventually becoming a Presbyterian minister in the early 1900s and beginning his evangelistic tours thereafter. A longtime affiliate of the YMCA and friends with its international secretary, John Mott, Sunday helped bring regional support to the ACASR in Syracuse and central New York. Through local secretary Almus Oliver, many individuals, including Azadian, Koolakian, and Philibosian, were in regular contact with Sunday during the early years of President Wilson's relief effort. Although Sunday was not a trustee of the later-organized ACIA, he played a role in the earliest meetings of this organization in 1919.

The year 1916 brought a large influx of immigrants into Syracuse and Onondaga County because of the war. The resultant strain on the social institutions of greater Syracuse prompted local educator and philanthropist T. Aaron Levy to form a new organization: the Syracuse and Onondaga County Americanization League. This organization provided regional immigration and naturalization services for the next sixty years through a central administration of case workers, each of them trained to represent their own ethnic nationality.

During the years 1916 to 1918, Azadian and Koolakian learned from the ACASR's national committee about the plight of an Armenian refugee girl.[70] Displaced from her home in Chmshkatsag, a town in the Mamuret ul-Aziz (Kharpert or Harpoot) province and orphaned as a result of the massacres, fifteen-year-old Arshalouis (Aurora) Mardiganian made her way to Erzerum, where she came under the care of local ACASR representatives. She was eventually brought to America under sponsorship of the ACASR national committee. While she was staying temporarily in a New York City hotel, the ACASR prompted her to write her autobiography, *Ravished Armenia* (known as *The Auction of Souls* in Great Britain), which was turned into a play and published in book form in 1919. Miss Mardiganian's account became the theme for a major movie production, *Ravished Armenia,* a seven-reel production in which she and Ambassador Morgenthau played key roles. The book, its play, and the motion picture (filmed by Metro Pictures Corporation), were underwritten by the ACASR/NER.[71] The proceeds helped to fund the thirty-million-dollar NER campaign in 1919 and 1920.[72]

Azadian, Koolakian, Philibosian, and the Syracuse committee assisted Arshalouis Mardiganian and the NER in the early stages of her work—most likely with translation. These gentlemen all had a fluent command of the Armenian and Turkish languages. Much of their work with the national committee was held in strict confidence to avoid premature and inaccurate publicity (see fig. 42 on page 89). A private viewing of *Ravished Armenia* was held at the Hotel Plaza auditorium the weekend of 7 February 1919.[73] It followed a joint meeting of the executive committees of the NER and the ACIA. Azadian and Koolakian were present that evening by invitation of the NER and by separate invitation of Ambassador James Gerard, chairman of the ACIA and former ambassador to Germany (see fig. 43 on page 90).

During the early period of Woodrow Wilson's Armenian-Syrian Relief Days, there was an effort to satisfy regional interest in the Armenian cause by distributing copies of Alice Stone Blackwell's book *Armenian Poems* (revised in 1917) (a poem from the book is in fig. 44 on page 91). The proceeds were funneled into the ACASR's national campaign. In a letter to Akabi Azadian, Blackwell expresses gratitude to the Azadians for their "efforts to arouse interest in the Armenian question" by means of her book.

From 1918 to 1920, the Syracuse ACASR/NER sponsored several regional fund-raisers in the performing arts, such as symphony orchestra concerts and plays, some of the latter produced in cooperation with the Syracuse branch of the Armenian Students' Association of America (established locally in 1915) and the Americanization League. Perhaps the most notable of these performances was *The Vartanantz,* a beautiful pageant in which many local residents, costumed in full regalia, reenacted the historic battle of Avarayr in A.D. 451 between the Persians and the Armenians (see fig. 45 on page 92).

The last performance on 12 September 1919, staged at the outdoor portico of the New York State fairgrounds, drew enough attention to merit a visit from the NER's national executive committee;[74] Dr. John H. Finley, executive publisher of the *New York Times* and trustee of the NER; and New York's governor, Alfred E. Smith, and his wife.[75] Governor Smith had been a supporter of the ACASR, and in December 1918, he became an executive committee member of the newly organized ACIA. Finley had recently been in Constantinople on an international assignment with the NER, returning to the United States in time to attend the NER-sponsored Armenian exhibit and pageant in Syracuse.

Fig. 35. Armenian and Syrian Relief banner and table placards. These were issued to commemorate the adoption of Woodrow Wilson's annual Armenian-Syrian Relief Days, which began nationwide by Congressional proclamation on the thirty-second anniversary of Edison Lamp Day, 21 October 1916. The banners were printed and distributed to members of the American Board of Commissioners for Foreign Missions, the American Committee for Armenian and Syrian Relief, and at fund-raising meetings beginning that day in New York City. It was no coincidence that the Association of Edison Illuminating Companies (headquartered in New York) gave its assistance to this effort because some of its most prominent affiliates actively supported the American Board and the Armenian and Syrian Relief program during this period.

AMERICAN COMMITTEE FOR ARMENIAN AND SYRIAN RELIEF

70 FIFTH AVENUE, NEW YORK

INCLUDING WORK OF THE ARMENIAN RELIEF, THE PERSIAN WAR RELIEF, AND THE SYRIAN-PALESTINE RELIEF COMMITTEES

JAMES L. BARTON	SAMUEL T. DUTTON	CHARLES V. VICKREY	CHARLES R. CRANE
CHAIRMAN	SECRETARY	EXECUTIVE SECRETARY	TREASURER

FREDERICK H. ALLEN	FRED B. FISHER	WOODBURY G. LANGDON	FRANK MASON NORTH	ISAAC N. SELIGMAN
ARTHUR J. BROWN	JAMES CARDINAL GIBBONS	FREDERICK LYNCH	HARRY V. OSBORNE	WILLIAM SLOANE
EDWIN M. BULKLEY	RT. REV. DAVID H. GREER	CHAS. S. MACFARLAND	GEORGE A. PLIMPTON	EDWARD LINCOLN SMITH
JOHN B. CALVERT	NORMAN HAPGOOD	H. PEREIRA MENDES	RT. REV. P. RHINELANDER	JAMES M. SPEERS
JOHN D. CRIMMINS	MAURICE H. HARRIS	WILLIAM B. MILLAR	KARL DAVIS ROBINSON	OSCAR S. STRAUS
CLEVELAND H. DODGE	WILLIAM I. HAVEN	JOHN MOFFAT	WILLIAM W. ROCKWELL	STANLEY WHITE
CHARLES W. ELIOT	HAMILTON HOLT	HENRY MORGENTHAU	WM. JAY SCHIEFFELIN	TALCOTT WILLIAMS
WILLIAM T. ELLIS	ARTHUR CURTISS JAMES	JOHN R. MOTT	GEORGE T. SCOTT	STEPHEN S. WISE

October 21, 1916.

Dear Co-worker:-

You have doubtless felt with the rest of us, the severe limitations of time in making satisfactory preparation for Armenian-Syrian Relief Days, as designated by the President, October 21st-22nd.

In many places it has been utterly impossible to secure the literature and prepare the public for an adequate response.

We write to ask if you cannot follow the plan that is being adopted in several cities, of regarding October 21-22 as days for the formal publication of the President's proclamation through press and pulpit, but with the understanding that a week or ten days following will be required to secure results.

Many people will not awake to the urgency of the need until the days designated by the President are past. Many influential citizens will not be present at church services and other places where the appeal is presented. An organized, systematic follow-up is imperative if adequate returns are to be secured.

To meet this situation many committees are arranging to use the next week or ten days for personal solicitation of prosperous citizens for substantial contributions, commensurate with the need. They will then supplement this personal solicitation by the preparation of longer lists of well-to-do citizens to whom will be sent with the assistance of a secretary or competent stenographer, personally addressed letters, asking for contributions.

A supply of the leaflet "The Cry of Millions" can be secured for enclosure with this letter and the expense of the circularization easily be met, preferably by individual members of the local committee, or if necessary, by the local treasurer from receipts.

The need is colossal and the help of all will be required to make provision for the approaching winter. A government collier is now being prepared to transport the first load of food stuffs. Other shipments must follow.

Command us if we can be of any assistance from this office.

Sincerely yours,

C. V. Vickrey

BY ACT OF CONGRESS AND PROCLAMATION OF THE PRESIDENT, ARMENIAN-SYRIAN RELIEF DAYS, OCT. 21-22

Fig. 36. Letter from Charles Vickrey to members of the American Committee for Armenian and Syrian Relief, 21 October 1916.

October 24, 1916.

Mr. George G. Koolakian, Esq.,
Jerry Rescue Building
Syracuse, N. Y.

My dear Mr. Koolakian:—

It was a pleasure hosting you and Mr. Philibosian
at our meeting in Manhattan on the Twenty-first to which
I thank you for your generous gift of $250.00 to the
Armenian-Syrian Relief Days. I have forwarded your check
drawn on the First National Bank with other contributions
from the Fourth Presbyterian Church, Syracuse to Mr.
Cleveland Dodge totaling $1,758.00. The dedicated work
of colleagues as yourselves has made our first program an
overwhelming success. It is to this urgent humanitarian
need that President Wilson's declaration was summoned into
service on Edison Lamp Day; need we say more about the
importance this international observance has represented
to the campaign? Syracuse's report is informative; the
delivery was excellent and your participation in the event
was outstanding.

I should congratulate you for all the fine work you
and the Church have contributed to our regional campaign,
but we know that our tidings are overshadowed in light of
your recent most unfortunate news. We deeply regret the
unexpected loss of your sister and family to the Armenian
massacres and pray you are comforted in knowing we are
doing everything possible to administer this humanitarian
program as expeditiously needed. Ambassador Morgenthau,
Mr. Dodge and I extend on behalf of all our members the
sincerest sympathies of the Armenian-Syrian Relief Committee. As Mr. Crane told you, we did not learn the
whereabouts of your family until news of their fate was
transmitted from our Office of Foreign Affairs in Beirut,
and only belatedly were those details confirmed.

With sincerest sympathy and admiration, I remain,

John W. Lieb
New York Committee

Fig. 37. Letter from John W. Lieb to George Koolakian, 24 October 1916. In the midst of George Koolakian's early regional work with the American Committee for Armenian and Syrian Relief, the ACASR's Near East Foreign Office informed the national organization of the tragic massacre of his sister, her family, and other members of Koolakian's family during their exile on the Armenian death marches beginning from their hometown region in the southern Marmora district in August 1915.

AMERICAN COMMITTEE FOR ARMENIAN AND SYRIAN RELIEF

JAMES L. BARTON, Chairman   SAMUEL T. DUTTON, Vice-Chairman   CHARLES V. VICKREY, Secretary   CLEVELAND H. DODGE, Treasurer

ONE MADISON AVENUE, NEW YORK

CABLE ADDRESS, LAYMEN   TELEPHONE, GRAMERCY, 1024

DEPOSITORY, NATIONAL CITY BANK, NEW YORK

H. C. JAQUITH
ASSISTANT SECRETARY   October 25, 1916.

Mr. George G. Koolakian
Custom Garment Making Company
Jerry Rescue Building
Syracuse, New York

My dear Mr. Koolakian:-

News has reached me from Mr. Cleveland Dodge of the unspeakable tragedy to your family sustained during the recent Armenian massacres in Turkey. I am deeply saddened and must write you.

Ambassador Morgenthau's experience in Constantinople is a vivid reminder that we are fortunate to live in these United States where freedom permits us to address the compelling need of others, and to lend relief through America's helping-hand. The war has opportuned these political convulsions in Turkey upon an innocent peace-abiding people. No matter how distant it may be, Armenia's affliction is a tragedy uniting the conviction of free citizens everywhere, and I cannot help but feel infinitely closer to it knowing you personally. Your loss is our loss; the compelling issue is central to the American Committee and its establishment.

We earnestly hope that America's continued support of this program will somehow ease your burden and the lot of so many Armenian-Americans who share your unfortunate fate. The world at-large cannot afford, nor can it justify wanton human destruction at any level, for the price we all must endure is incalculable. America must ever seek to instill this civility in others. It is our mission and democratic responsibility.

My heart goes out to you and the members of your family to-day with the desire that our expanded undertaking will have lasting benefit in restoring peace and justice in these troubled times.

I should like to call upon you and Mr. Azadian to discuss some confidential matters when I am in Syracuse.

I remain in our humanitarian work with esteem and empathy.

Yours sincerely,

Wm. Howard Taft

Wm. Howard Taft

Fig. 38. Letter from William Howard Taft to George Koolakian, 25 October 1916. This personal letter written to Koolakian by the ACASR National Committee member William Howard Taft, the former president of the United States, is a poignant reminder of the devastation wrought by the "wanton human destruction," and the reason underlying the establishment of the nationwide ACASR/NER program, which soon attracted millions of American supporters. These sentiments soon gave rise to the Armenian independence movement in the years between 1918 and 1920 and expressed a level of social and political concern for a minority people that arguably exceeded that of any previous era in American history.

REFUGEES ARRIVE AT HAVEN AFTER 2,000-MILE WALK

Family of Peter Roomian, Syracuse, in Band of Persecuted Armenians.

SENT FROM CONSTANTINOPLE

Goaded by Turkish Guards During Long Journey to Jerusalem.

MANY DIE BY THE ROADSIDE

Letter, First News Received from Relatives Since War Began, Tells of Sufferings of Deported People.

A story of sufferings endured by deported Armenians on their more than 2,000-mile journey by foot from Constantinople to Jerusalem has been written by Miss Kayzne Roomian to her brother, Peter Roomian, No. 214 Harrison street.

The letter contains the first word Mr. Roomian has received from his family since the war began. He read in a newspaper that the people of the small village where his family lived near Constantinople had been deported, but all efforts to obtain further news of them had been unavailing.

30 Months on Journey.

Miss Roomian's letter has been more than two months on the way from Jerusalem. It tells a tale of horrors during the thirty months the little group of unfortunate people were making their journey. Mr. Roomian's father, mother, three sisters and two brothers were in the deported band. All the family arrived safely in Jerusalem.

"We are here and safe, but there is not much of us but our bones," the young woman wrote. "My pen can not write the horrors we have endured on the way. Out of every hundred that left Constantinople with us only five have reached this city.

"The Turkish police who were our guards and who rode horseback as we walked, practiced every form of cruelty. The sick were killed with knives when they grew too weak to walk further. Those who were old and for this reason unable to keep up with the marchers were left to die by the roadside. We were never allowed to rest in towns or cities. Always we must take what rest we had in the open country.

Little Rest Permitted.

"We had but little clothing when we left, as we were allowed to take with us only what we could carry. We were in desperate plight long before we reached Jerusalem. We were pushed on and on the guard allowing us as little time as possible for rest.

"When we finally reached here it was just after the British had taken the city and we thanked God. For now we can see a ray of hope, tho we do not know what is to be done with us or where we will be sent from here.

"We are now living in a church, as many of our people as can be gotten into the building. We are thankful for such food as the British can provide. They are doing their best for the refugees."

Mr. Roomian has been in this country nearly five years. When he left his home his family was in fairly prosperous circumstances, owning their own home. The sister who wrote was receiving a salary as teacher of French in the Armenian school. He is making every effort to send help to his people.

Fig. 39. Article in the *Syracuse Post-Standard* of 31 March 1918 relating Peter Roomian's sister's tale of survival.

Fig. 40. Rotary Club of Syracuse, meeting in the Hotel Onondaga Roof Garden, ca. 1916. The Rotary Club contributed significantly to the regional American Committee for Armenian and Syrian Relief (ACASR) and Near East Relief (NER) fund-raising and clothing drives, working with the Syracuse Businessmen's Association (predecessor of the Syracuse Chamber of Commerce), the Liberty Loan Committee, the Young Men's Christian Association, and the Syracuse Masonic Temple. Convening weekly in the once-famous Hotel Onondaga Roof Garden on East Jefferson Street, the Rotary held many public service events during the war years and beyond. Harutun Azadian, New York State assembly leader Thaddeus Sweet, George Koolakian, and T. Aaron Levy are seated at the front table on the left in the foreground.

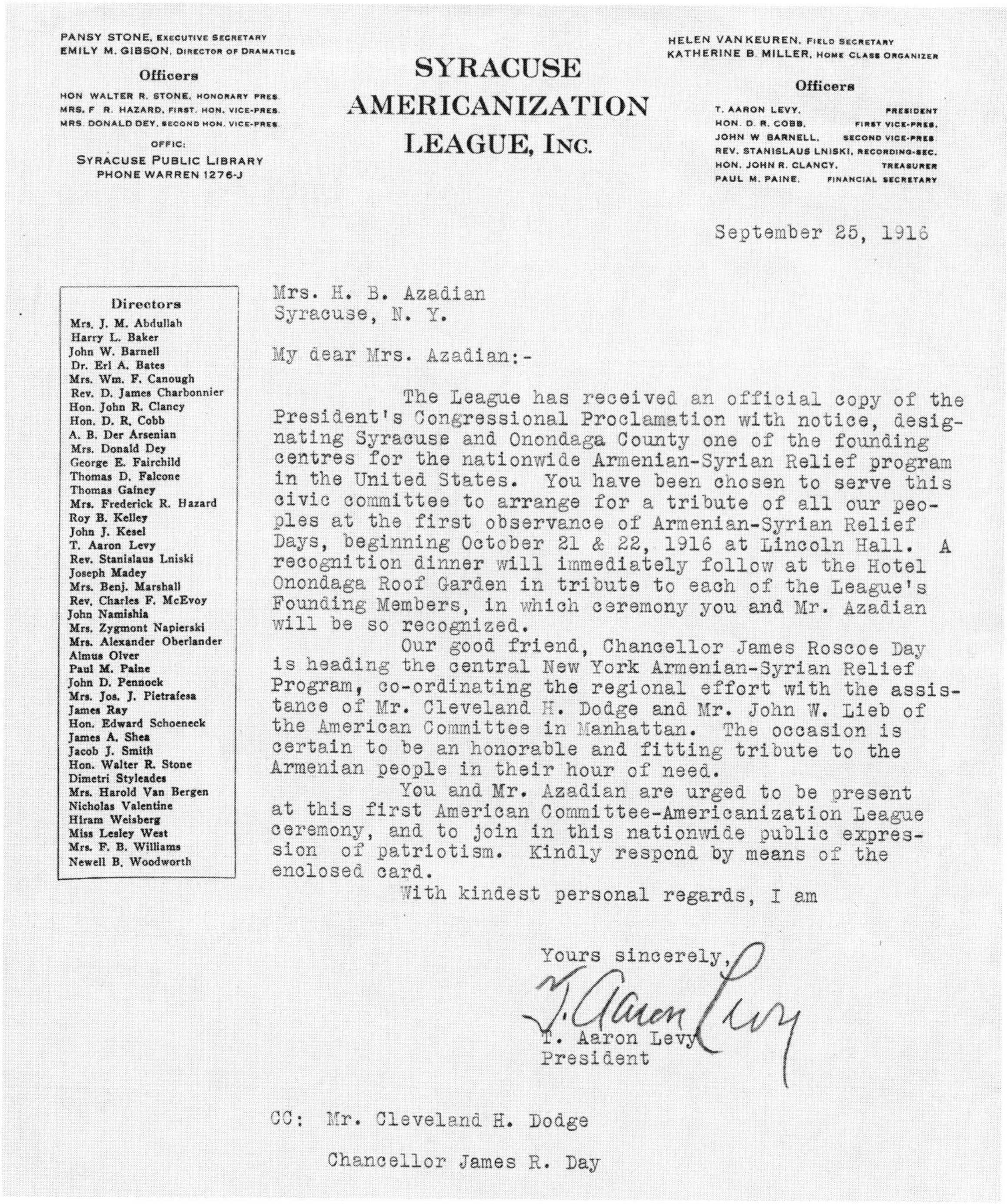

PANSY STONE, EXECUTIVE SECRETARY
EMILY M. GIBSON, DIRECTOR OF DRAMATICS

Officers

HON WALTER R. STONE, HONORARY PRES.
MRS. F R. HAZARD, FIRST. HON. VICE-PRES.
MRS. DONALD DEY, SECOND HON. VICE-PRES.

OFFIC:
SYRACUSE PUBLIC LIBRARY
PHONE WARREN 1276-J

SYRACUSE AMERICANIZATION LEAGUE, INC.

HELEN VANKEUREN, FIELD SECRETARY
KATHERINE B. MILLER, HOME CLASS ORGANIZER

Officers

T. AARON LEVY, PRESIDENT
HON. D. R. COBB, FIRST VICE-PRES.
JOHN W BARNELL, SECOND VICE-PRES.
REV. STANISLAUS LNISKI, RECORDING-SEC.
HON. JOHN R. CLANCY, TREASURER
PAUL M. PAINE, FINANCIAL SECRETARY

Directors

Mrs. J. M. Abdullah
Harry L. Baker
John W. Barnell
Dr. Erl A. Bates
Mrs. Wm. F. Canough
Rev. D. James Charbonnier
Hon. John R. Clancy
Hon. D. R. Cobb
A. B. Der Arsenian
Mrs. Donald Dey
George E. Fairchild
Thomas D. Falcone
Thomas Gafney
Mrs. Frederick R. Hazard
Roy B. Kelley
John J. Kesel
T. Aaron Levy
Rev. Stanislaus Lniski
Joseph Madey
Mrs. Benj. Marshall
Rev. Charles F. McEvoy
John Namishia
Mrs. Zygmont Napierski
Mrs. Alexander Oberlander
Almus Olver
Paul M. Paine
John D. Pennock
Mrs. Jos. J. Pietrafesa
James Ray
Hon. Edward Schoeneck
James A. Shea
Jacob J. Smith
Hon. Walter R. Stone
Dimetri Styleades
Mrs. Harold Van Bergen
Nicholas Valentine
Hiram Weisberg
Miss Lesley West
Mrs. F. B. Williams
Newell B. Woodworth

September 25, 1916

Mrs. H. B. Azadian
Syracuse, N. Y.

My dear Mrs. Azadian:-

The League has received an official copy of the President's Congressional Proclamation with notice, designating Syracuse and Onondaga County one of the founding centres for the nationwide Armenian-Syrian Relief program in the United States. You have been chosen to serve this civic committee to arrange for a tribute of all our peoples at the first observance of Armenian-Syrian Relief Days, beginning October 21 & 22, 1916 at Lincoln Hall. A recognition dinner will immediately follow at the Hotel Onondaga Roof Garden in tribute to each of the League's Founding Members, in which ceremony you and Mr. Azadian will be so recognized.

Our good friend, Chancellor James Roscoe Day is heading the central New York Armenian-Syrian Relief Program, co-ordinating the regional effort with the assistance of Mr. Cleveland H. Dodge and Mr. John W. Lieb of the American Committee in Manhattan. The occasion is certain to be an honorable and fitting tribute to the Armenian people in their hour of need.

You and Mr. Azadian are urged to be present at this first American Committee-Americanization League ceremony, and to join in this nationwide public expression of patriotism. Kindly respond by means of the enclosed card.

With kindest personal regards, I am

Yours sincerely,

T. Aaron Levy

T. Aaron Levy
President

CC: Mr. Cleveland H. Dodge

Chancellor James R. Day

Fig. 41. Letter from T. Aaron Levy to Akabi Azadian, 25 September 1916. A significant boost in chartering the Syracuse Americanization League was experienced with the early input and support of the nationwide American Committee for Armenian and Syrian Relief, headquartered in New York City. Soon this organization achieved status as the Syracuse and Onondaga County Americanization League, a nonprofit immigration and naturalization service that provided assistance for the next sixty years. The prominent involvement of James Roscoe Day, the Syracuse University chancellor, is evident in documents such as this.

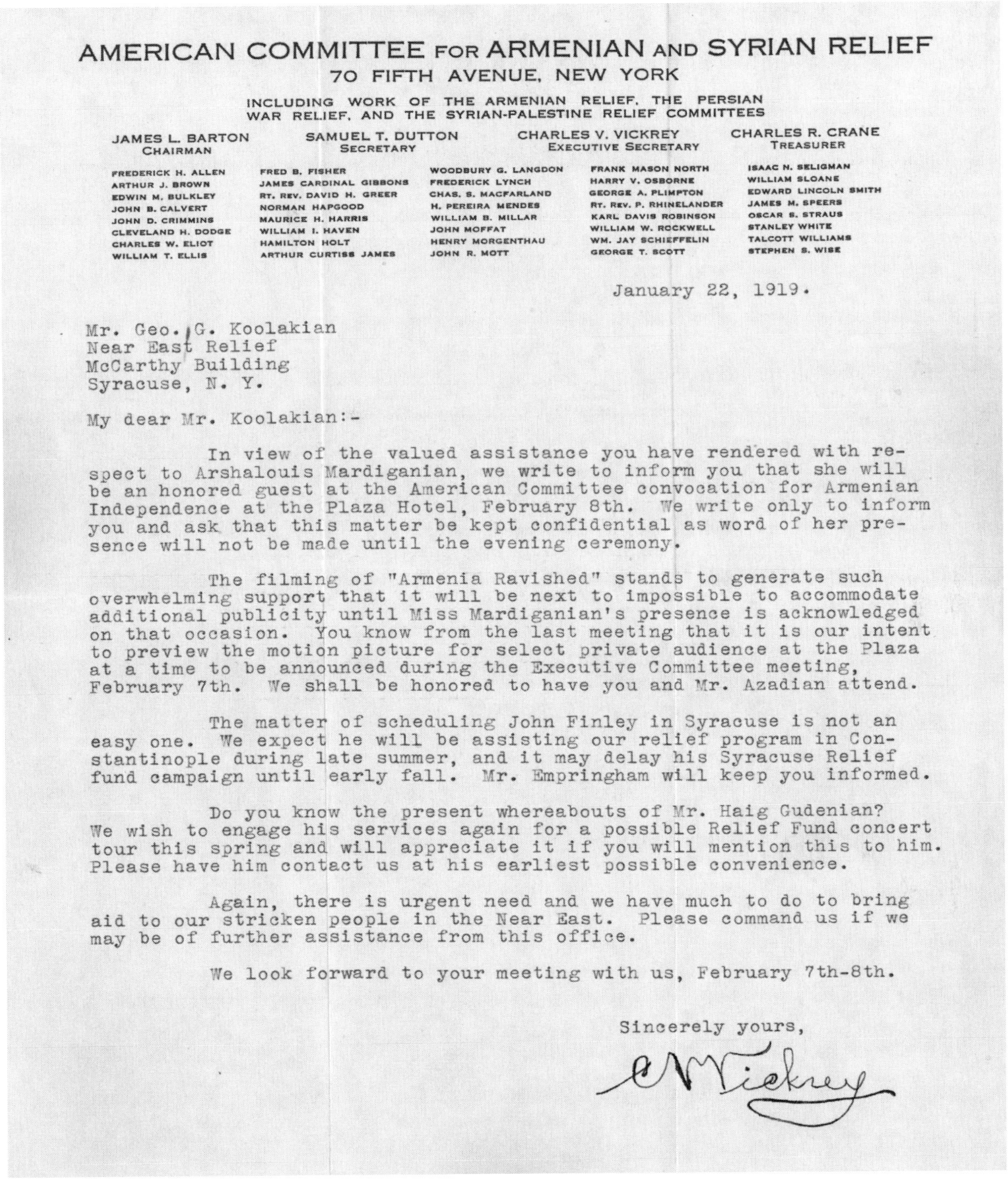

AMERICAN COMMITTEE FOR ARMENIAN AND SYRIAN RELIEF
70 FIFTH AVENUE, NEW YORK
INCLUDING WORK OF THE ARMENIAN RELIEF, THE PERSIAN WAR RELIEF, AND THE SYRIAN-PALESTINE RELIEF COMMITTEES

JAMES L. BARTON, CHAIRMAN — SAMUEL T. DUTTON, SECRETARY — CHARLES V. VICKREY, EXECUTIVE SECRETARY — CHARLES R. CRANE, TREASURER

January 22, 1919.

Mr. Geo. G. Koolakian
Near East Relief
McCarthy Building
Syracuse, N. Y.

My dear Mr. Koolakian:-

In view of the valued assistance you have rendered with respect to Arshalouis Mardiganian, we write to inform you that she will be an honored guest at the American Committee convocation for Armenian Independence at the Plaza Hotel, February 8th. We write only to inform you and ask that this matter be kept confidential as word of her presence will not be made until the evening ceremony.

The filming of "Armenia Ravished" stands to generate such overwhelming support that it will be next to impossible to accommodate additional publicity until Miss Mardiganian's presence is acknowledged on that occasion. You know from the last meeting that it is our intent to preview the motion picture for select private audience at the Plaza at a time to be announced during the Executive Committee meeting, February 7th. We shall be honored to have you and Mr. Azadian attend.

The matter of scheduling John Finley in Syracuse is not an easy one. We expect he will be assisting our relief program in Constantinople during late summer, and it may delay his Syracuse Relief fund campaign until early fall. Mr. Empringham will keep you informed.

Do you know the present whereabouts of Mr. Haig Gudenian? We wish to engage his services again for a possible Relief Fund concert tour this spring and will appreciate it if you will mention this to him. Please have him contact us at his earliest possible convenience.

Again, there is urgent need and we have much to do to bring aid to our stricken people in the Near East. Please command us if we may be of further assistance from this office.

We look forward to your meeting with us, February 7th-8th.

Sincerely yours,

C V Vickrey

Fig. 42. Letter from Charles Vickrey to George Koolakian, 22 January 1919.

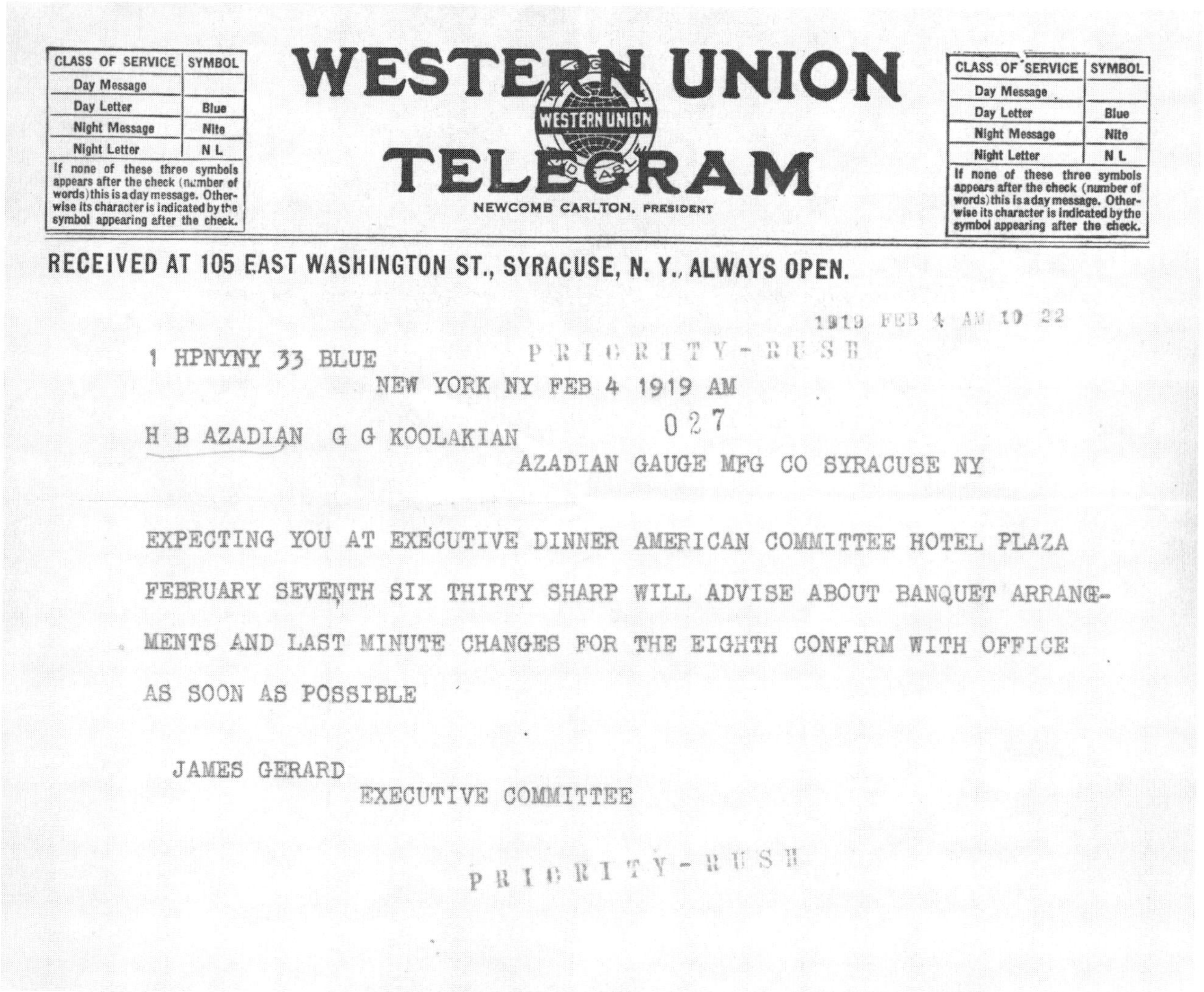

WESTERN UNION TELEGRAM

NEWCOMB CARLTON, PRESIDENT

CLASS OF SERVICE	SYMBOL
Day Message	
Day Letter	Blue
Night Message	Nite
Night Letter	N L

If none of these three symbols appears after the check (number of words) this is a day message. Otherwise its character is indicated by the symbol appearing after the check.

CLASS OF SERVICE	SYMBOL
Day Message	
Day Letter	Blue
Night Message	Nite
Night Letter	N L

If none of these three symbols appears after the check (number of words) this is a day message. Otherwise its character is indicated by the symbol appearing after the check.

RECEIVED AT 105 EAST WASHINGTON ST., SYRACUSE, N. Y., ALWAYS OPEN.

1919 FEB 4 AM 10 22

1 HPNYNY 33 BLUE   PRIORITY-RUSH

NEW YORK NY FEB 4 1919 AM

H B AZADIAN   G G KOOLAKIAN   0 2 7

AZADIAN GAUGE MFG CO SYRACUSE NY

EXPECTING YOU AT EXECUTIVE DINNER AMERICAN COMMITTEE HOTEL PLAZA

FEBRUARY SEVENTH SIX THIRTY SHARP WILL ADVISE ABOUT BANQUET ARRANGE-

MENTS AND LAST MINUTE CHANGES FOR THE EIGHTH CONFIRM WITH OFFICE

AS SOON AS POSSIBLE

JAMES GERARD

EXECUTIVE COMMITTEE

PRIORITY-RUSH

Fig. 43. Telegram from James Gerard to Harutun Azadian and George Koolakian, 4 February 1919.

Armenia in Mourning

Mother Armenia

(From the Armenian of Arshag Tchobanian)

All naked at crossroads thou dost sit,
The snow descends and clings along thine hair;
Dark wounds are in thy flesh; thine eyes have grown
As red as lakes of blood, in thy despair.

The ancient Mother thou, of age-long griefs;
Misfortune round thy heart its chain hath laid
In countless rings; black winds have smitten thee,
And heavy shadows on thy life have weighed.

Lift up thy head, weep not! Holy is grief
And great and wholesome. Earth naught noble knows
Than is the victim brave beneath his cross.
'Tis in the shadow that the dawn-light grows.

Trans. by Alice Stone Blackwell.

Fig. 44. Broadside entitled *Armenia in Mourning*, with lithographed background view of the mountains of Ararat. Alice Stone Blackwell translated the poem "Mother Armenia" by Arshag Tchobanian into English. In the years 1915 and 1916, the broadside was widely distributed by the American Board of Commissioners for Foreign Missions and the American Committee for Armenian and Syrian Relief as a way to promote public awareness of the Armenian situation.

Fig. 45. Armenian pageant at the New York State Fair in 1919. During Woodrow Wilson's presidency, Near East Relief and other organizations such as the Armenian Students' Association of America, sponsored several cultural events in Syracuse to benefit Armenians. In a pageant entitled *The Vartanantz,* local Armenians reenacted the historic battle of Avarayr, fought between the ancient Persians and Armenians on the plains of Ararat on 26 May in A.D. 451. Daily performances, which took place from 7 through 12 September 1919 in the outdoor portico at the New York State Fair, were attended by many public figures, including Governor Alfred E. Smith, as well as trustees of the American Board of Commissioners for Foreign Missions and Near East Relief. This photograph, taken at the concluding performance, includes, left to right: Hajirakpar Gebelian, Apraham Kurdian, Setrak Kalebdjian, Sam Minasian, Krikor Aghaian, Dikran Desteian, George Koolakian, Krikor Apikian, Hazaros Choghanjian, Misak Kalebdjian, Haig Koolakian, Mary Philibosian, Vahram Rejebian, Zarouhi Zahrajian, John Enfijian, John H. Finley, and Yervant Keledjian. The battle of Avarayr is considered to be the first of the "Holy Wars" waged in defense of Christianity and a day signifying religious freedom to the Armenians.

CHAPTER EIGHT
A NEW AMERICAN COMMITTEE

During the war, several Armenophile organizations were formed throughout the diaspora to promote the independence of Armenia. Among those in the United States were the Armenian National Union of America, the Armenian Colonial Association, and the Armenian Democratic League. The Armenian Revolutionary Federation, which had established itself in the eastern United States in 1894, also substantially enlarged its following. However, none became as influential as the ACIA, established in November and December 1918. Unlike all the others, the leaders of the ACIA were non-Armenian (see fig. 46 on page 97). Gregory Aftandilian, a chronicler of the ACIA movement, had this commentary:

> At the close of the war, Armenians throughout the world believed that because of their sufferings and sacrifices, the time had finally come to render justice to their aspirations. At least one third of the Armenian people had been destroyed by genocide, tens of thousands more by the war itself, and Armenian lands had been devastated. If this was the era of self-determination, of justice and humanity, then no other people had a more legitimate reason to expect the creation of a sovereign state. Never again would they be under the rule of the Turk.[76]

This sentiment was shared then by many American and world leaders. Through the American Committee for the Independence of Armenia, a remarkable cross-section of prominent Americans expressed concern for Armenian security and freedom in the immediate post-war era. In his book entitled *The Story of Near East Relief,* James L. Barton credits the formation of the ACASR/NER to the American Board of Commissioners for Foreign Missions.[77] While published sources fail to explain the inception of the ACIA, printed rosters reveal that the ACIA in turn was largely made up of ABCFM and ACASR/NER trustees. The first official roster of the ACIA, dated December 1918, lists the names of many high-level Americans—none of them Armenians. Azadian, Koolakian, and Philibosian became involved as confidential liaisons in the organization on the strength of their associations with the ABCFM and the ACASR/NER.[78] While there is no evidence to suggest that these three engaged in policymaking or structuring of the new organization, their participation followed that of prominent trustees of the ABCFM and the NER, such as Cleveland H. Dodge, Charles V. Vickrey, James L. Barton, Alice Stone Blackwell, and Elihu Root, who joined the executive or general committees of the ACIA in December 1918.

The Azadian-Koolakian memorabilia dated the first six weeks of 1919 indicate the participation in the ACIA of Wilson's cabinet members and congressional advisors, including some who served as advisors to or members of the American delegation to the Paris Peace Conference (see fig. 47 on page 98). However, little evidence of their participation appears among the fragmentary surviving records of the ACIA or among the effects of its later crusader, Vahan Cardashian, New York lawyer and champion of the Armenian cause. Dr. James H. Tashjian, former editor of the *Armenian Review* and publisher of Cardashian's papers, maintained that Azadian and Koolakian were regional correspondents for the ACIA during the earliest days of the Armenian independence movement, when few records were retained, other than those directly affecting the central office in New York City.[79] According to Tashjian, this dearth of documentation was a result of the loosely structured nature of the organization.[80]

The Azadian and Koolakian papers not only supplement and further explain the Cardashian papers, they also reveal the complex nature of the first Armenian independence movement in America during its earliest stages, as well as its relationship to other agencies and organizations. In a letter to Rev. James Roscoe Day (cofounder of central New York's ACASR), Charles Vickrey, the first national executive secretary of the NER, expresses high regard for Azadian, Koolakian, and Philibosian:

> November 17, 1918
>
> Rev. James R. Day
> American Committee for Armenian and Syrian Relief
> McCarthy Building
> Syracuse, New York
>
> My dear Colleague:
>
> . . . We have reviewed your recommendations. Thank you for offering the services of the Syracuse Orchestra to benefit our Relief campaign. This is a sacrifice for the new program, however, it is all to the call of the stricken Armenians. I fear for them but know we are doing everything in God's service to ease their undue sufferings.
>
> Let me state again that I believe the only fitting answer to this greatest of human tragedies is the democratic sovereignty of historical Armenia. This, of course, is not my conclusion, it is the respected judgement of every one of our colleagues who have responded to Armenian and Syrian Relief from the beginning. Barton, Dodge, and Peet are now concluding a formal request, a recommendation to go before President Wilson on behalf of Armenian independence and may I state as a matter of course that it is long overdue. If there is anything that can inure to the greater benefit of these industrious people, I do not know of it. They need to be free and independent, to be left alone to work [out] their own destiny. We hope that humankind shall not bear witness to another tragedy as the Armenian, and that our effort to secure a future for these God-fearing people by virtue of their respected civilization will not be in vain. The world must not forget them.

I appeal to you on another aspect as regards Armenian independence. . . . [W]ill you kindly advise Azadian, Koolakian, and Philibosian of this pending matter, in the likelihood they are called into service. We already have substantial experience with them and they have responded with utmost trustworthiness and confidence.

Yours in his work.
Sincerely
Charles V. Vickrey[81]

The petition mentioned in the letter above was transmitted from "Messrs. Barton, Dodge and Peet" to Secretary of State Robert Lansing, who sent it to the president's secretary, Joseph Tumulty, on 22 November 1918. Tumulty, in turn, placed the petition into the official presidential record, and it is acknowledged in *The Papers of Woodrow Wilson*.[82]

Historians have also failed to acknowledge that administrative members of the United States War Industries and Naval Consulting boards also helped to found the ACIA (see fig. 48 on page 99). Both of these boards were created by executive order during Woodrow Wilson's first term. He had a close relationship with their chief officers, War Industries Board chairman Bernard M. Baruch and naval secretary Josephus Daniels. Azadian and Koolakian had had contact with these two through their prior work with the ABCFM and the ACASR/NER. Azadian, in particular, had known Baruch and Daniels through extensive government contract work that he and his firm, the Azadian Gauge Manufacturing Company, had done for both boards and many of their members. One of America's few precision instrument makers, Azadian was well regarded among the Washington technocrats of the day (see fig. 49 on page 100).

Reasons for the involvement of the two war boards in the early affairs of the ACIA are not readily apparent, but it stands to reason that President Wilson would want Baruch and Daniels involved. They were not only advisors to the president on domestic and international issues, but Wilson had also appointed them as principal advisors to the Paris Peace Conference of 1919 and 1920.

Before the conference, conditions for Armenian independence looked especially favorable. After much fighting to defend from a Turkish onslaught a small part of its historical territory, which had been in the Russian Empire, Armenia formally declared its independence at the end of May 1918. With the end of the war in November, Armenia's fate as a struggling democracy would lie in the hands of the Western world at the bargaining table.

Americans who had been exposed to news of the Turkish atrocities against the Armenians for more than four years were strongly in favor of Armenian independence. Many remembered the massacres between 1894 and 1896 when some two hundred thousand innocent Armenians had lost their lives. The massacres that began in March 1915, which took an additional one and one-half million lives, only served to intensify American public resolve.

Wilson went to the Paris conference weeks before its official opening on 18 January 1919, and was absent from the United States for more than two and one-half months. The conference was to be the testing ground for implementing his Fourteen Point program, with its guiding principle that "the world must be made safe for democracy." He had labored for several weeks with his cabinet advisors on this program—first made public in January 1918—and on the proposed League of Nations, the forerunner of the United Nations. The Fourteen Points addressed political and territorial issues that had been left unresolved by the Congress of Berlin in 1878. Point twelve was now interpreted as a call for the establishment of an independent Armenia, with its historical boundaries.

The American Committee for the Independence of Armenia

EXECUTIVE COMMITTEE
James W. Gerard, *Chairman*

Charles Evans Hughes
Elihu Root
Henry Cabot Lodge
John Sharp Williams

Alfred E. Smith
Frederick Courtland Penfield
Charles W. Eliot
Cleveland H. Dodge

GENERAL COMMITTEE
Charles Evans Hughes, *Honorary Chairman*
James W. Gerard, *Chairman*

William Jennings Bryan
Alton B. Parker
Elihu Root
Henry Cabot Lodge
John Sharp Williams
Charles S. Thomas
Lyman Abbott
Gov. Bartlett, N.H.
James L. Barton
Gov. Beeckman, R.I.
Alice Stone Blackwell
Charles J. Bonaparte
Gov. Boyle, Nev.
Nicholas Murray Butler
Gov. Campbell, Ariz.
Gov. Carey, Wyo.
Gov. Catts, Fla.
Gov. Cooper, S.C.
Gov. Cox, Ohio
Charles Stewart Davison
Rt. Rev. J. H. Darlington
Cleveland H. Dodge
Gov. Dorsey, Ga.
Charles W. Eliot
Rt. Rev. William F. Faber
Admiral Bradley A. Fiske
Lindley M. Garrison
James Cardinal Gibbons
Martin H. Glynn
Samuel Gompers
Madison Grant
Lloyd C. Griscom
Gov. Harding, Iowa
Gov. Harrington, Md.
Albert Bushnell Hart
Sara Duryea Hazen
Myron T. Herrick

John Grier Hibben
Gov. Holcomb, Conn.
Hamilton Holt
George A. Hurd
Richard M. Hurd
Henry W. Jessup
Robert Ellis Jones
Gov. Larrazolo, N. Mex.
Gov. Lister, Wash.
Edward C. Little
Julian W. Mack
Norman E. Mack
William T. Manning
Elizabeth Marbury
Rt. Rev. Wm. H. Moreland
Gov. Norbeck, S. Dak.
Frederic C. Penfield
George Haven Putnam
Rt. Rev. P. N. Rhinelander
Ernest W. Riggs
Wm. Henry Roberts
Gov. Robertson, Okla.
Jacob G. Schurman
Gov. Smith, N.Y.
Gov. Sproul, Pa.
Oscar S. Straus
Rt. Rev. A. C. Thompson
Gov. Townsend, Jr., Del.
Rt. Rev. B. D. Tucker
Rt. Rev. Wm. W. Webb
Benjamin Ide Wheeler
Everett P. Wheeler
Rt. Rev. J. R. Winchester
Stephen S. Wise
Gov. Withycombe, Ore.
Gov. Yager, Puerto Rico

Fig. 46. The first official roster of the American Committee for the Independence of Armenia (ACIA), December 1918. Representing most of the forty-eight states and U.S. territories, these participants were also involved in the American Board of Commissioners for Foreign Missions and the American Committee for Armenian and Syrian Relief. Some of them were even in the state department during the early months of the Paris Peace Conference (1919–20), when public support for the democratic emancipation of Armenia was at an all-time high in America. Note that no Armenians are listed as executive committee or general committee members (see note 78 for more information).

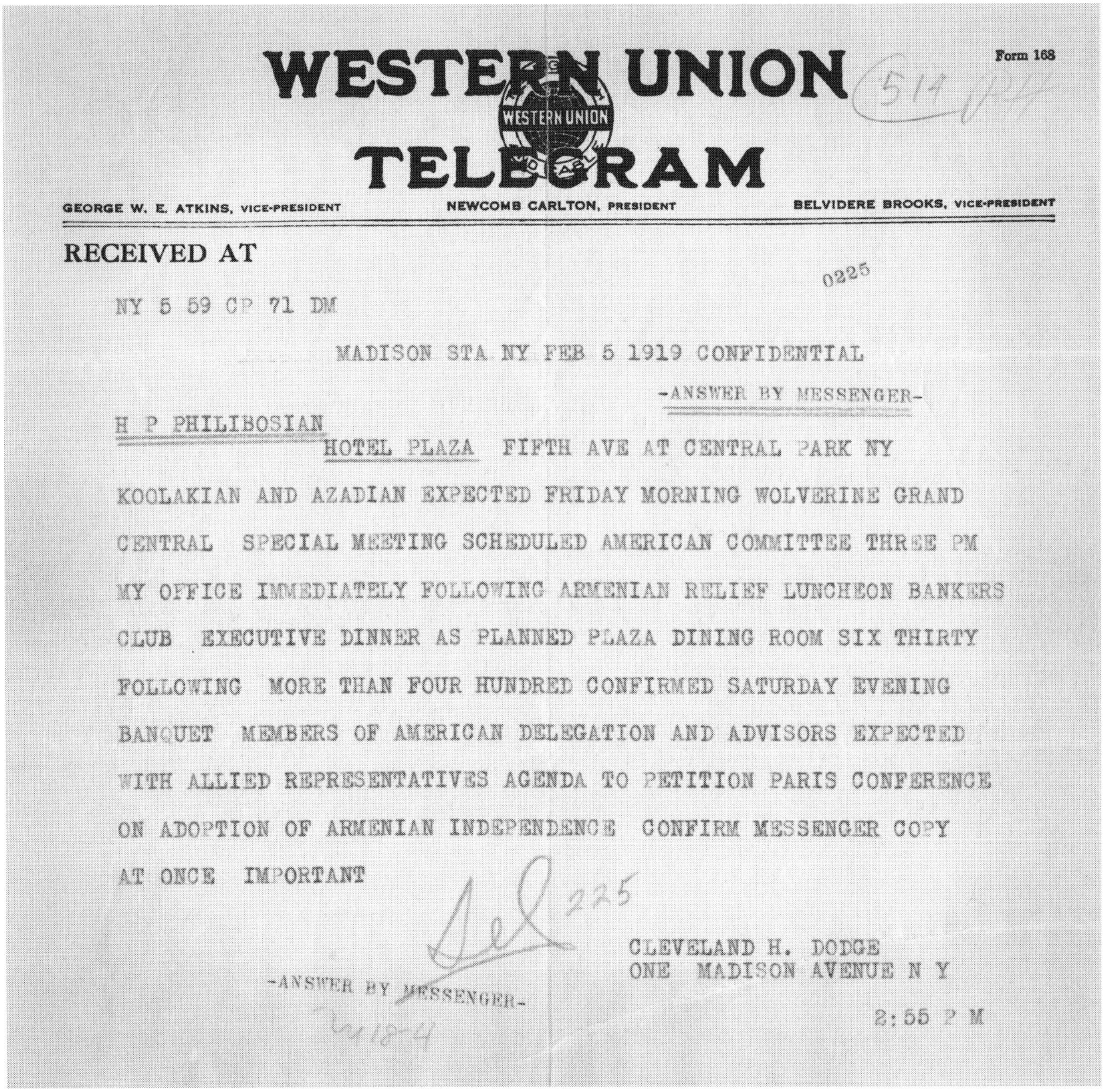

WESTERN UNION TELEGRAM

Form 168

(514)

GEORGE W. E. ATKINS, VICE-PRESIDENT   NEWCOMB CARLTON, PRESIDENT   BELVIDERE BROOKS, VICE-PRESIDENT

RECEIVED AT

0225

NY 5 59 CP 71 DM

MADISON STA NY FEB 5 1919 CONFIDENTIAL

-ANSWER BY MESSENGER-

H P PHILIBOSIAN

HOTEL PLAZA FIFTH AVE AT CENTRAL PARK NY

KOOLAKIAN AND AZADIAN EXPECTED FRIDAY MORNING WOLVERINE GRAND
CENTRAL SPECIAL MEETING SCHEDULED AMERICAN COMMITTEE THREE PM
MY OFFICE IMMEDIATELY FOLLOWING ARMENIAN RELIEF LUNCHEON BANKERS
CLUB EXECUTIVE DINNER AS PLANNED PLAZA DINING ROOM SIX THIRTY
FOLLOWING MORE THAN FOUR HUNDRED CONFIRMED SATURDAY EVENING
BANQUET MEMBERS OF AMERICAN DELEGATION AND ADVISORS EXPECTED
WITH ALLIED REPRESENTATIVES AGENDA TO PETITION PARIS CONFERENCE
ON ADOPTION OF ARMENIAN INDEPENDENCE CONFIRM MESSENGER COPY
AT ONCE IMPORTANT

225

CLEVELAND H. DODGE
ONE MADISON AVENUE N Y

-ANSWER BY MESSENGER-

2:55 P M

Fig. 47. Telegram from Cleveland H. Dodge to Harutun P. Philibosian, 5
February 1919.

Fig. 48. Members of the United States War Industries Board in the summer of 1918, soon after the board's restructuring by Woodrow Wilson. From left to right are Thomas A. Edison (in the foreground); Henry Ford; Bernard Baruch; George Eastman (standing behind Baruch, with only his hat showing); Arshalouis Azadian (talking with Eastman); Owen D. Young (wearing a hat), the vice president and soon-to-be chairman of General Electric Company and the Radio Corporation of America; Josephus Daniels (in profile), naval secretary and chairman of the Naval Consulting Board; and Harutun B. Azadian (without a hat and facing the camera over Daniels's left shoulder). Azadian often advised and sometimes traveled with these American captains of industry. They were supportive of President Wilson's Near East relief programs and of the Armenian independence movement at the close of World War I. Courtesy of Arshalouis Azadian Randall.

Fig. 49. Photograph taken in the experimental design and testing laboratory of the Azadian Gauge Manufacturing Company in Syracuse during a typical work session in 1913. It was here that Azadian produced the prototype of the "planetary" transmission for local manufacturer William H. Brown and Henry Ford in the spring of 1908. The testing of the device was conducted for Brown, Ford, and Charles Steinmetz for installation in Ford's first production of the Model T automobile in the fall of that year. This information is corroborated in Alexander Brown's "Recollections of William H. Brown" in the Syracuse Masonic Temple records and cites the early collaborative involvement (1899) of George Hine, Harutun B. Azadian, William H. Brown, and Charles Steinmetz in Azadian's gauge block work and the later collaboration (1906–9) of Brown, Azadian, Steinmetz, and Henry Ford in die work, prototype design, and the manufacture of transmissions for the Ford Motor Company. (From left to right are Benjamin Dudukian, Arthur M. Fichter, Mihran Danielian, and Jewel W. Vanderveer. In the background from the left are Ely A. Bodour, Lloyd W. Moulton, Valentine J. Metzger, Knodel Strandel, Harutun Azadian (with his arm on the flywheel), and John B. West. Azadian's factory was remembered as a congenial meeting place where inventors and technicians often came to discuss ideas and to work on experimental designs. Many immigrants in the Syracuse area began their employment here. All Brown memorabilia, unless otherwise specified, is in the Azadian Collection.

CHAPTER NINE
THE FIRST CONVENTION OF THE AMERICAN COMMITTEE FOR THE INDEPENDENCE OF ARMENIA

Documents in the Azadian-Koolakian collection show that the period from early January through late February 1919 was a particularly important time. Preparations for the ACIA inaugural were under way, and citizens at the highest political and social levels were discussing the Armenian situation. The following discussion represents a brief chronology of some of the more important Azadian and Koolakian documents.

Early in January 1919, ACIA executive committee member Elihu Root addressed an invitation to his friend and former cabinet chief, Theodore Roosevelt, who had been a supporter of the ABCFM and the ACASR/NER. Roosevelt, the 1905 winner of the Nobel Peace Prize who had sought to forge a new global role for America during the Spanish-American War, now devoted considerable effort to seeking justice for the Armenian people. On 5 January 1919, he responded by telegram to Azadian and Koolakian through the NER (see fig. 50 on page 106).[83]

Few individuals knew that the Roosevelt family and several members of his former presidential cabinet were expected to participate in the new organization. Azadian and Koolakian had met Roosevelt in upstate New York during his 1912 presidential campaign.[84] They had had later contact with him through their regional work with the NER. Based on this telegram and other documents, it is apparent that Azadian and Koolakian were responsible for coordinating the attendance of certain people in their region on behalf of the NER and the ACIA. It must have been a sad day when they learned that Roosevelt had passed away unexpectedly in his sleep during the early morning hours of 6 January 1919—on the occasion of Armenian Christmas.[85] In spite of their recent loss, his wife, Edith Carow Roosevelt; two daughters, Alice Roosevelt Longworth and Ethel Roosevelt; Roosevelt's sister Corinne Roosevelt Robinson; his sister-in-law, Sarah Roosevelt,; and, by some accounts, his cousin Eleanor Roosevelt attended the 8 February inaugural ceremony.

On 8 January 1919, a day letter from William Jennings Bryan to Koolakian provided information about the upcoming ACIA convention (see fig. 51 on page 107). On 11 January, a few days after Roosevelt's death, Azadian and Koolakian received a dispatch from naval secretary Josephus Daniels (see fig. 52 on page 108). These telegrams illustrate the significance the convention held for the Allies as they began post-war negotiations at the Paris Peace Conference.

On 15 January, Azadian received a telegram from Thomas A. Edison, who had been an active member of both the Naval Consulting and War Industries boards.[86] Apparently, the Edison family invitation had occasioned a discussion of the Armenian question between the inventor and War Industries Board chairman Bernard Baruch (see fig. 53 on page 109). Although Edison himself was not known to have been there, other members of the Sloane-Edison family were present, including Mrs. Mina M. Edison; Madeleine Edison (Mrs. John) Sloane,[87] the inventor's daughter; and Carolyn Hawkins (Mrs. Charles) Edison.[88] In addition, Dr. John W. Lieb was there. Lieb, an Edison Pioneer of early distinction and a prominent member of the New York charter committee of the ACASR/NER, was an early supporter of the Armenian independence movement.[89]

George Eastman wired Azadian on 19 January 1919 at the latter's gauge company. An old friend of George Eastman, Azadian had produced die work and gauging systems for Eastman Kodak during its early years. Later, Koolakian and Philibosian were associated with Eastman through his support of the NER. It was most likely through the Azadian-Eastman friendship and their subsequent affiliation with the War Industries Board that Eastman came to sympathize with the Armenian independence movement (see fig. 54 on page 110).

By 22 January 1919, the order of events for the banquet had been formulated and agreed upon—except for a few later modifications—by members of the banquet planning committee, which included Charles V. Vickrey, Charles Stewart Davison, James Watson Gerard, and Henry Morgenthau. Two days earlier, on 20 January, Ambassador Gerard and Charles S. Davison—among several other signatories to the original ACIA petition—had sent a cable to President Wilson in Paris via the state department, informing him of the status of the 8 February ACIA convention banquet and requesting a letter from him to be read during the proceedings.[90]

On 4 February, Ambassador James Gerard wired a telegram to Azadian and Koolakian confirming their expected attendance at the ACIA's executive committee planning dinner on the evening of Friday, 7 February (see fig. 43 on page 90). This executive committee dinner at the Hotel Plaza was to mark the beginning of the inaugural ACIA convention.

Azadian and Koolakian left Syracuse by train for New York City early in the morning on Friday, 7 February 1919.[91] With Mrs. Azadian accompanying them, they arrived at the Plaza Hotel in time to confirm their weekend itinerary. It began with an afternoon luncheon sponsored by the NER's National Committee and hosted at the Bankers' Club in Manhattan, near the hotel. The purpose of that gathering was to recognize regional NER field workers from throughout the United States and to review their involvement in the first segment of the ACASR/NER's recently announced thirty-million-dollar national fund-raising campaign. The participants expressed a profound desire to seek justice for the Armenian people.

Dr. Stephen S. Wise, cofounder of Near East Relief and trustee of the newly formed ACIA, had recently returned to New York from meetings with Woodrow Wilson at the Paris Peace Conference. Obviously moved by his experience at the conference, and by the president's effort to secure democratic independence for Armenia, Dr. Wise addressed the luncheon guests with these enthusiastic words:

> It is only a few days since my return from Paris and I saw something of what was going on there. Your hearts should rejoice, as my heart rejoices, in the circumstance that the leader of the American people stands out above all other men as the leader of the world in the direction of peace through justice. He has come to command the reverence and the affection and the faith of millions

of men who do not speak the English tongue, but who understand him, who love him and honor him because they feel that he is, as we believe him to be, America incarnate.

And now I have come to share good tidings with you. . . . We believe that the day of liberation for Armenia must come soon, that Armenia is at least to be free to weave its own destiny. It may be that Armenia will accept or agree to accept some trusteeship or guarantee, which will not limit, but safeguard her from harm. I know that Armenia is grateful for all that America has done for her during these terrible years. Perhaps we, or the world, will forget what she has gone through, but Armenia will never forget.

Let me say that, for this help, we have to thank the Armenian and Syrian Committee for Relief in the Near East, whose leader . . . we all cherish and love. We must remember two things— we must keep Armenia from Turkish iniquity, and then we must feed her.[92]

Stephen Wise and other speakers that afternoon told of plans for ending Turkish rule in Armenia, Syria, and Palestine and for establishing a new democratic government in Armenia under proper safeguards and guarantees. It was reported by the various NER team leaders that from New York City alone more than one million dollars had been raised for Armenian Relief. New York representatives said that within the next seventy-two hours they would make an unprecedented effort to raise an additional million dollars, and, indeed, they did—a remarkable philanthropic achievement for that time.[93]

The executive committee dinner was held in the Plaza's executive dining room beginning at 6:30 that evening. This session was attended, and probably cochaired, by NER executive secretary Charles V. Vickrey and ACIA chairman James Gerard. Vickrey had preconfirmed these arrangements (with Koolakian) on 22 January. Ambassador Gerard had done so in a separate reminder sent to Azadian and Koolakian on 4 February 1919.[94]

Following the dinner meeting, a "select private audience" (NER and ACIA executives and invited guests) watched a preview of the NER-sponsored motion picture *Armenia Ravished*. Arshalouis [Aurora] Mardiganian starred in the leading role in her autobiographical production.

George Eastman was present at that preview not only because he supported the ACASR/NER and the Armenian independence movement, but also because his invention of continuous flexible celluloid film and the establishment of the Eastman film industry made him a founder of the National Motion Picture Association, the very organization selected by the NER to undertake the seven-reel Armenian documentary. The press failed to acknowledge his presence, along with many other important aspects of the inaugural weekend. Historians have also ignored the fact that Eastman played an important part in NER events between 1915 and 1920.[95]

The *New York Times* published a review of *Armenia Ravished*, which had its debut one week later in the Plaza auditorium and, publicly, at the Hotel Commodore. Mrs. Oliver Harriman and Mrs. George Vanderbilt of the

National Motion Picture Committee presided over that event, the Harriman and Vanderbilt families being prominent supporters of the NER and of Armenian independence.[96] According to the review, Mrs. Harriman introduced the film in this manner:

> Miss Mardiganian had come to this country because she was a typical case selected from among her people as one of the many victims of the terrible desolation wrought in Armenia by the Turk. The whole purpose of the [motion] picture is to acquaint America with ravished Armenia to visualize conditions so that there will be no misunderstanding in the mind of anyone about the terrible things which have transpired. It was deemed essential that the leaders, social and intellectual, should first learn the story, but later the general public shall be informed. It is proposed that before this campaign of information is completed, as many adults as possible shall know the story of Armenia and the screen was selected as the medium because it reaches the millions where the printed word reaches the thousands.[97]

Returning to the Hotel Plaza by way of Cleveland Dodge's office at One Madison Avenue in time to prepare for the executive committee dinner, Azadian, Koolakian, and Philibosian were handed three Western Union messages.[98] They are chronicled in the order of their arrival (see figs. 55, 56, and 57 on pages 111, 112, and 113).

The first message, from President Wilson, is among the most important documents in the Azadian-Koolakian Papers. Wilson was not present at the inaugural weekend due to his attendance at the peace conference.[99]

The second message, from Bernard Baruch, places Azadian and Koolakian's interorganizational involvement into perspective.[100] It is evident that they were not only liaisons for the ACIA, but were also associated with the American delegation, receiving direction from Baruch, an important member of the American Commission to Negotiate Peace.

The last of the three Western Union communications was from Charles Steinmetz. All three messages expressed optimism that the Paris Peace Conference would result in Armenian independence.

When the Friday afternoon NER luncheon meeting was concluding at the Bankers Club, Charles S. Davison, one of the NER's afternoon participants, directed another internal telegram to the acting secretary of state on behalf of the ACIA (see fig. 58 on page 114).

State department officials were involved in the ACIA from the time of the original petition drawn up by Dr. James L. Barton, Cleveland H. Dodge, and W. W. Peet on 22 November 1918. In fact, few details regarding the ACIA escaped state department scrutiny. Its officers had been responsible for assembling the first membership roster of this new post-war organization. It can be inferred from Davison's telegram that the inaugural convention banquet had been planned from the inception of the ACIA late in 1918 by same nucleus of "eminent Americans" who were signatories to the original petition (see the executive committee and general committee roster of the ACIA (see fig. 46 on page 97). It is also apparent that the state department was aware in advance that "the American Committee for the Independence of Armenia [was to] hold a banquet on the eighth day of February in advocacy of its [of the signers'] purpose," and that the intent had already won support from "the Allied Governments."

Based on the sheer number of interrelated state department records about the ACIA (also called the American Commission for Armenian Independence), it can be concluded that the organization was regarded as an important initiative. It was part of the department's postwar American Commission to Negotiate Peace, with its multifaceted responsibility toward the settlement not only of Armenia, but also of Greece, Turkey, Bulgaria, Romania, Serbia, Croatia, Montenegro, Albania, Poland, and the territory of the former Austro-Hungarian Empire, as well as that of Belgium and Germany. Two of the ACIA's leading members—Charles Evans Hughes and William Jennings Bryan—the keynote speakers at its first convention banquet on 8 February 1919, confirmed the primacy of Armenia's independence as an example of the democratic rebuilding of the entire affected region.

Considering the stature and influence of the people invited to the inaugural ACIA convention, it is understandable that the state department and the military were involved. Their plan was for the banquet held at the Hotel Plaza that weekend to become known as the official beginning of the ACIA—but not until news of that festive occasion had been disclosed by the press, after the fact, on Sunday, 9 February 1919.

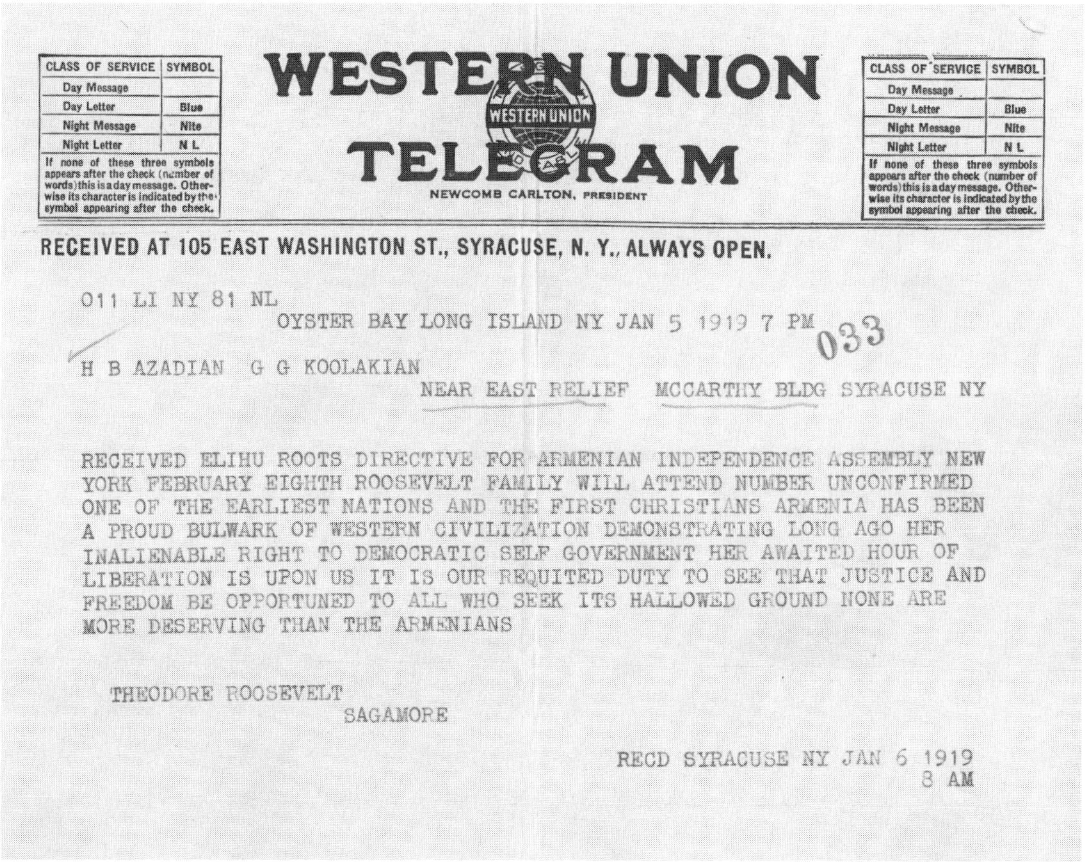

WESTERN UNION
TELEGRAM
NEWCOMB CARLTON, PRESIDENT

CLASS OF SERVICE	SYMBOL
Day Message	
Day Letter	Blue
Night Message	Nite
Night Letter	N L

If none of these three symbols appears after the check (number of words) this is a day message. Otherwise its character is indicated by the symbol appearing after the check.

CLASS OF SERVICE	SYMBOL
Day Message	
Day Letter	Blue
Night Message	Nite
Night Letter	N L

If none of these three symbols appears after the check (number of words) this is a day message. Otherwise its character is indicated by the symbol appearing after the check.

RECEIVED AT 105 EAST WASHINGTON ST., SYRACUSE, N. Y., ALWAYS OPEN.

011 LI NY 81 NL

OYSTER BAY LONG ISLAND NY JAN 5 1919 7 PM 033

H B AZADIAN   G G KOOLAKIAN

NEAR EAST RELIEF   MCCARTHY BLDG SYRACUSE NY

RECEIVED ELIHU ROOTS DIRECTIVE FOR ARMENIAN INDEPENDENCE ASSEMBLY NEW
YORK FEBRUARY EIGHTH ROOSEVELT FAMILY WILL ATTEND NUMBER UNCONFIRMED
ONE OF THE EARLIEST NATIONS AND THE FIRST CHRISTIANS ARMENIA HAS BEEN
A PROUD BULWARK OF WESTERN CIVILIZATION DEMONSTRATING LONG AGO HER
INALIENABLE RIGHT TO DEMOCRATIC SELF GOVERNMENT HER AWAITED HOUR OF
LIBERATION IS UPON US IT IS OUR REQUITED DUTY TO SEE THAT JUSTICE AND
FREEDOM BE OPPORTUNED TO ALL WHO SEEK ITS HALLOWED GROUND NONE ARE
MORE DESERVING THAN THE ARMENIANS

THEODORE ROOSEVELT
      SAGAMORE

RECD SYRACUSE NY JAN 6 1919
                    8 AM

Fig. 50. Telegram from Theodore Roosevelt to Harutun Azadian and George Koolakian, 5 January 1919.

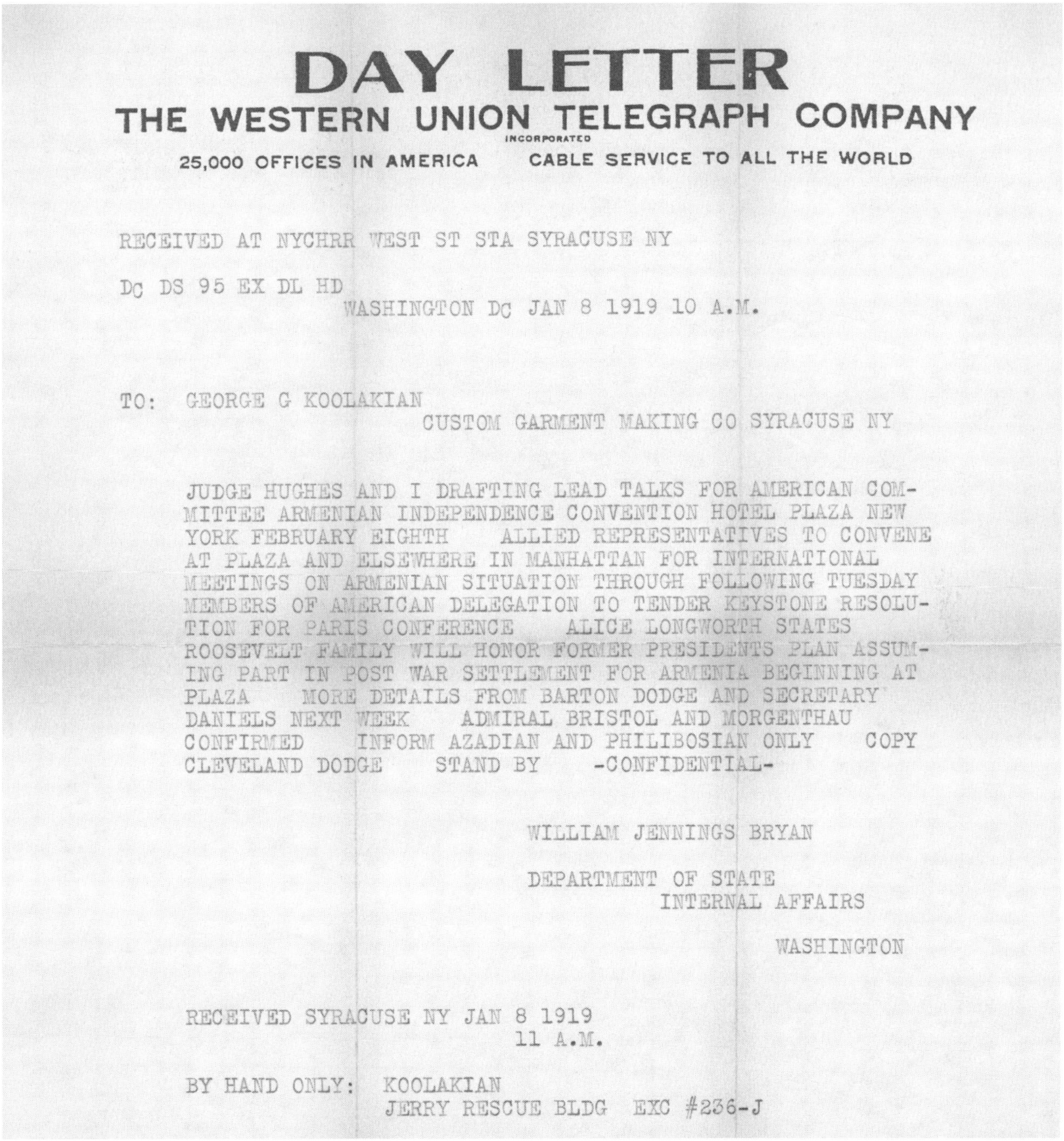

DAY LETTER
THE WESTERN UNION TELEGRAPH COMPANY
INCORPORATED
25,000 OFFICES IN AMERICA   CABLE SERVICE TO ALL THE WORLD

RECEIVED AT NYCHRR WEST ST STA SYRACUSE NY

DC DS 95 EX DL HD
               WASHINGTON DC JAN 8 1919 10 A.M.

TO: GEORGE G KOOLAKIAN
                    CUSTOM GARMENT MAKING CO SYRACUSE NY

JUDGE HUGHES AND I DRAFTING LEAD TALKS FOR AMERICAN COM-
MITTEE ARMENIAN INDEPENDENCE CONVENTION HOTEL PLAZA NEW
YORK FEBRUARY EIGHTH   ALLIED REPRESENTATIVES TO CONVENE
AT PLAZA AND ELSEWHERE IN MANHATTAN FOR INTERNATIONAL
MEETINGS ON ARMENIAN SITUATION THROUGH FOLLOWING TUESDAY
MEMBERS OF AMERICAN DELEGATION TO TENDER KEYSTONE RESOLU-
TION FOR PARIS CONFERENCE   ALICE LONGWORTH STATES
ROOSEVELT FAMILY WILL HONOR FORMER PRESIDENTS PLAN ASSUM-
ING PART IN POST WAR SETTLEMENT FOR ARMENIA BEGINNING AT
PLAZA   MORE DETAILS FROM BARTON DODGE AND SECRETARY
DANIELS NEXT WEEK   ADMIRAL BRISTOL AND MORGENTHAU
CONFIRMED   INFORM AZADIAN AND PHILIBOSIAN ONLY   COPY
CLEVELAND DODGE   STAND BY   -CONFIDENTIAL-

                    WILLIAM JENNINGS BRYAN

                    DEPARTMENT OF STATE
                          INTERNAL AFFAIRS

                                WASHINGTON

RECEIVED SYRACUSE NY JAN 8 1919
                11 A.M.

BY HAND ONLY: KOOLAKIAN
               JERRY RESCUE BLDG   EXC #236-J

Fig. 51. "Day Letter" from William Jennings Bryan to George Koolakian, 8 January 1919. This is one of the most important documents in the Azadian-Koolakian holdings because it establishes the involvement of the state department in the earliest activities of the ACIA and the confidential treatment with which the matter of Armenian independence was being handled by the government. Bryan and Henry Morgenthau were brought into the national leadership of the ACASR/NER (1915) and into the ACIA (December 1918) upon its organization and prior to its founding convention on 7 and 8 February 1919.

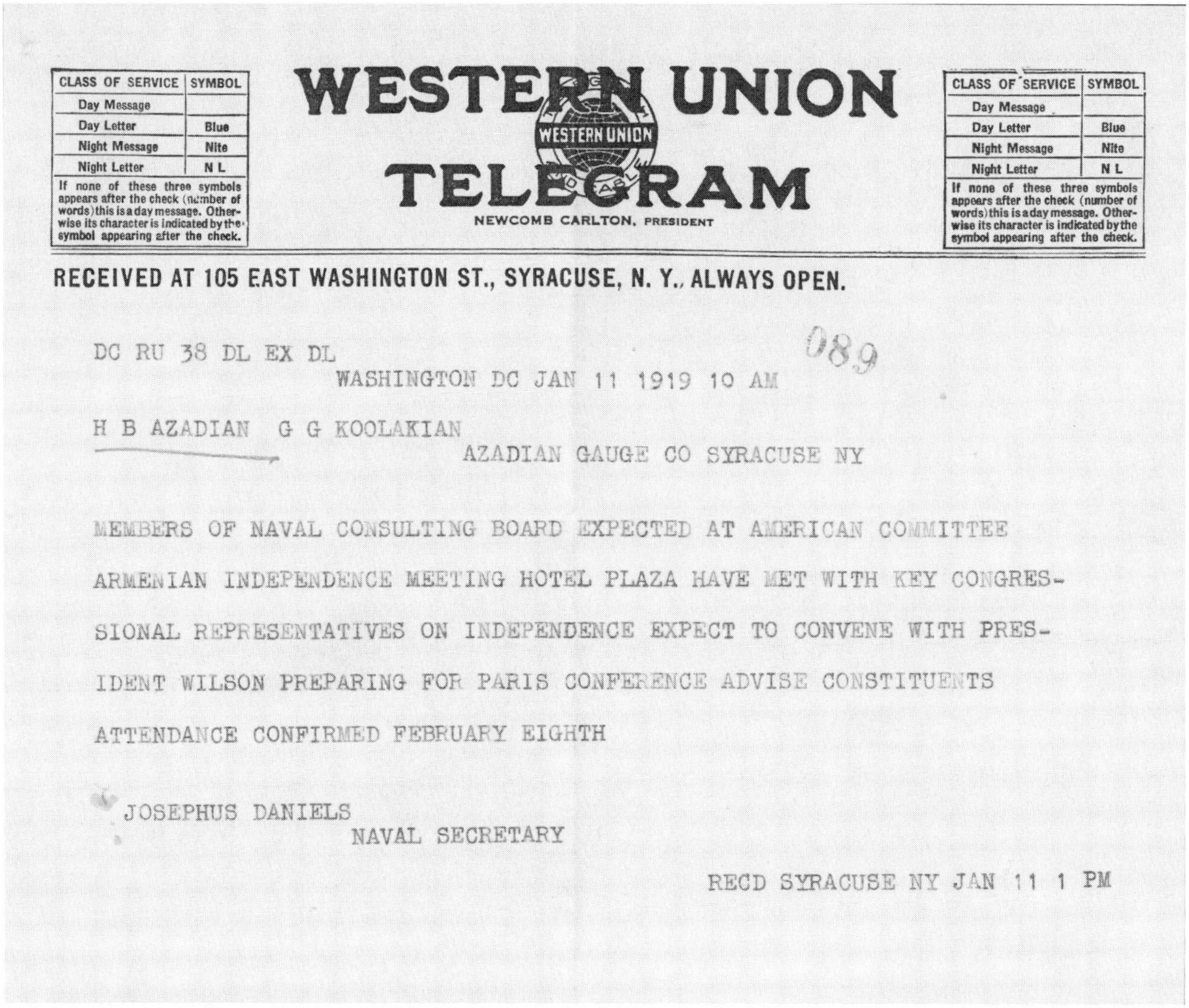

WESTERN UNION TELEGRAM

NEWCOMB CARLTON, PRESIDENT

CLASS OF SERVICE	SYMBOL
Day Message	
Day Letter	Blue
Night Message	Nite
Night Letter	N L

If none of these three symbols appears after the check (number of words) this is a day message. Otherwise its character is indicated by the symbol appearing after the check.

CLASS OF SERVICE	SYMBOL
Day Message	
Day Letter	Blue
Night Message	Nite
Night Letter	N L

If none of these three symbols appears after the check (number of words) this is a day message. Otherwise its character is indicated by the symbol appearing after the check.

RECEIVED AT 105 EAST WASHINGTON ST., SYRACUSE, N. Y., ALWAYS OPEN.

DC RU 38 DL EX DL

089

WASHINGTON DC JAN 11 1919 10 AM

H B AZADIAN G G KOOLAKIAN

AZADIAN GAUGE CO SYRACUSE NY

MEMBERS OF NAVAL CONSULTING BOARD EXPECTED AT AMERICAN COMMITTEE
ARMENIAN INDEPENDENCE MEETING HOTEL PLAZA HAVE MET WITH KEY CONGRES-
SIONAL REPRESENTATIVES ON INDEPENDENCE EXPECT TO CONVENE WITH PRES-
IDENT WILSON PREPARING FOR PARIS CONFERENCE ADVISE CONSTITUENTS
ATTENDANCE CONFIRMED FEBRUARY EIGHTH

JOSEPHUS DANIELS
        NAVAL SECRETARY

RECD SYRACUSE NY JAN 11 1 PM

Fig. 52. Telegram from Josephus Daniels to Harutun Azadian and George
Koolakian, 11 January 1919.

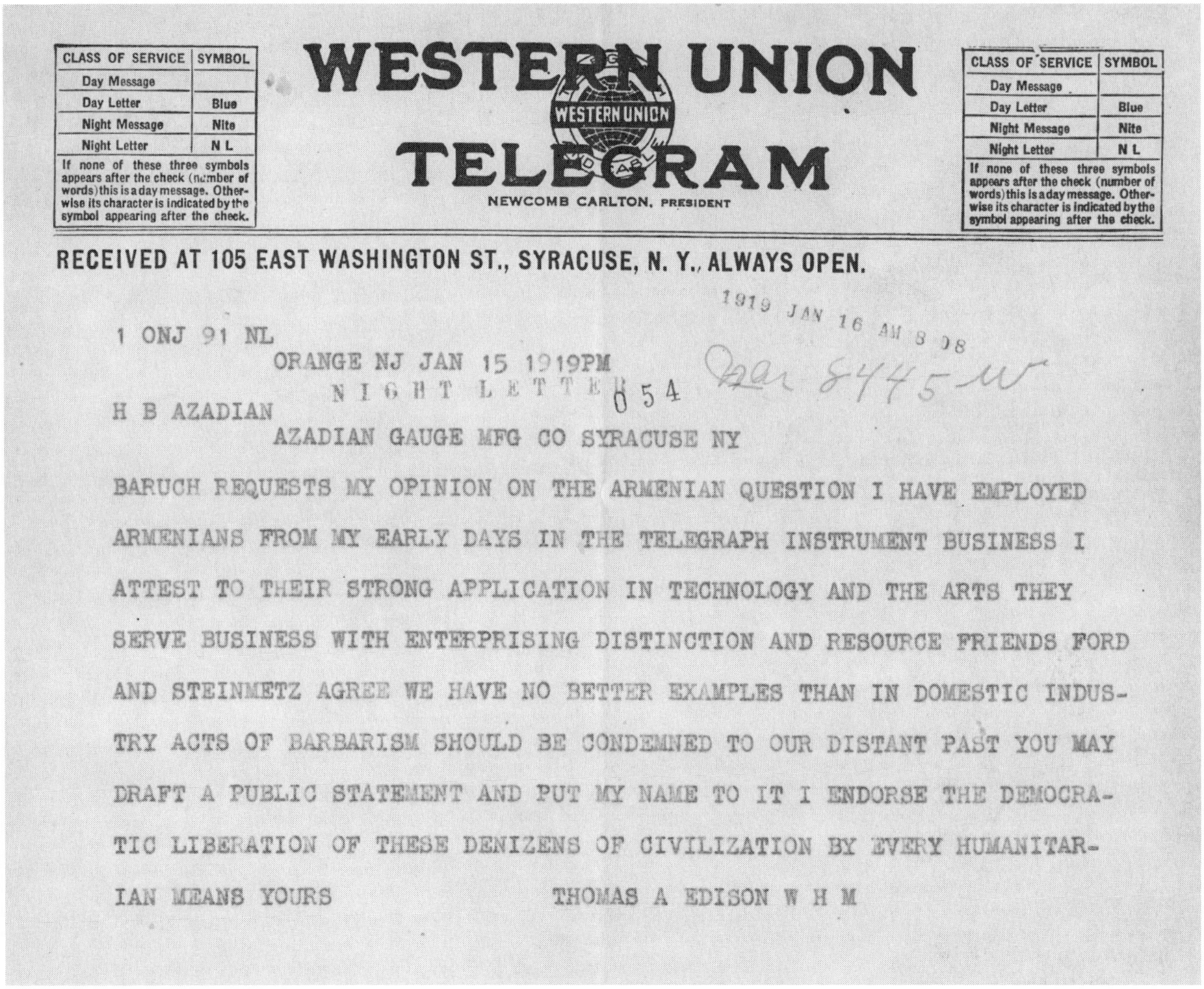

CLASS OF SERVICE | SYMBOL
Day Message |
Day Letter | Blue
Night Message | Nite
Night Letter | N L

If none of these three symbols appears after the check (number of words) this is a day message. Otherwise its character is indicated by the symbol appearing after the check.

WESTERN UNION
TELEGRAM

NEWCOMB CARLTON. PRESIDENT

CLASS OF SERVICE | SYMBOL
Day Message |
Day Letter | Blue
Night Message | Nite
Night Letter | N L

If none of these three symbols appears after the check (number of words) this is a day message. Otherwise its character is indicated by the symbol appearing after the check.

RECEIVED AT 105 EAST WASHINGTON ST., SYRACUSE, N. Y., ALWAYS OPEN.

1919 JAN 16 AM 8 08

1 ONJ 91 NL

ORANGE NJ JAN 15 1919PM

NIGHT LETTER 054

H B AZADIAN

AZADIAN GAUGE MFG CO SYRACUSE NY

BARUCH REQUESTS MY OPINION ON THE ARMENIAN QUESTION I HAVE EMPLOYED
ARMENIANS FROM MY EARLY DAYS IN THE TELEGRAPH INSTRUMENT BUSINESS I
ATTEST TO THEIR STRONG APPLICATION IN TECHNOLOGY AND THE ARTS THEY
SERVE BUSINESS WITH ENTERPRISING DISTINCTION AND RESOURCE FRIENDS FORD
AND STEINMETZ AGREE WE HAVE NO BETTER EXAMPLES THAN IN DOMESTIC INDUS-
TRY ACTS OF BARBARISM SHOULD BE CONDEMNED TO OUR DISTANT PAST YOU MAY
DRAFT A PUBLIC STATEMENT AND PUT MY NAME TO IT I ENDORSE THE DEMOCRA-
TIC LIBERATION OF THESE DENIZENS OF CIVILIZATION BY EVERY HUMANITAR-
IAN MEANS YOURS   THOMAS A EDISON W H M

Fig. 53. Telegram from Thomas A. Edison to Harutun Azadian, 15 January 1919.

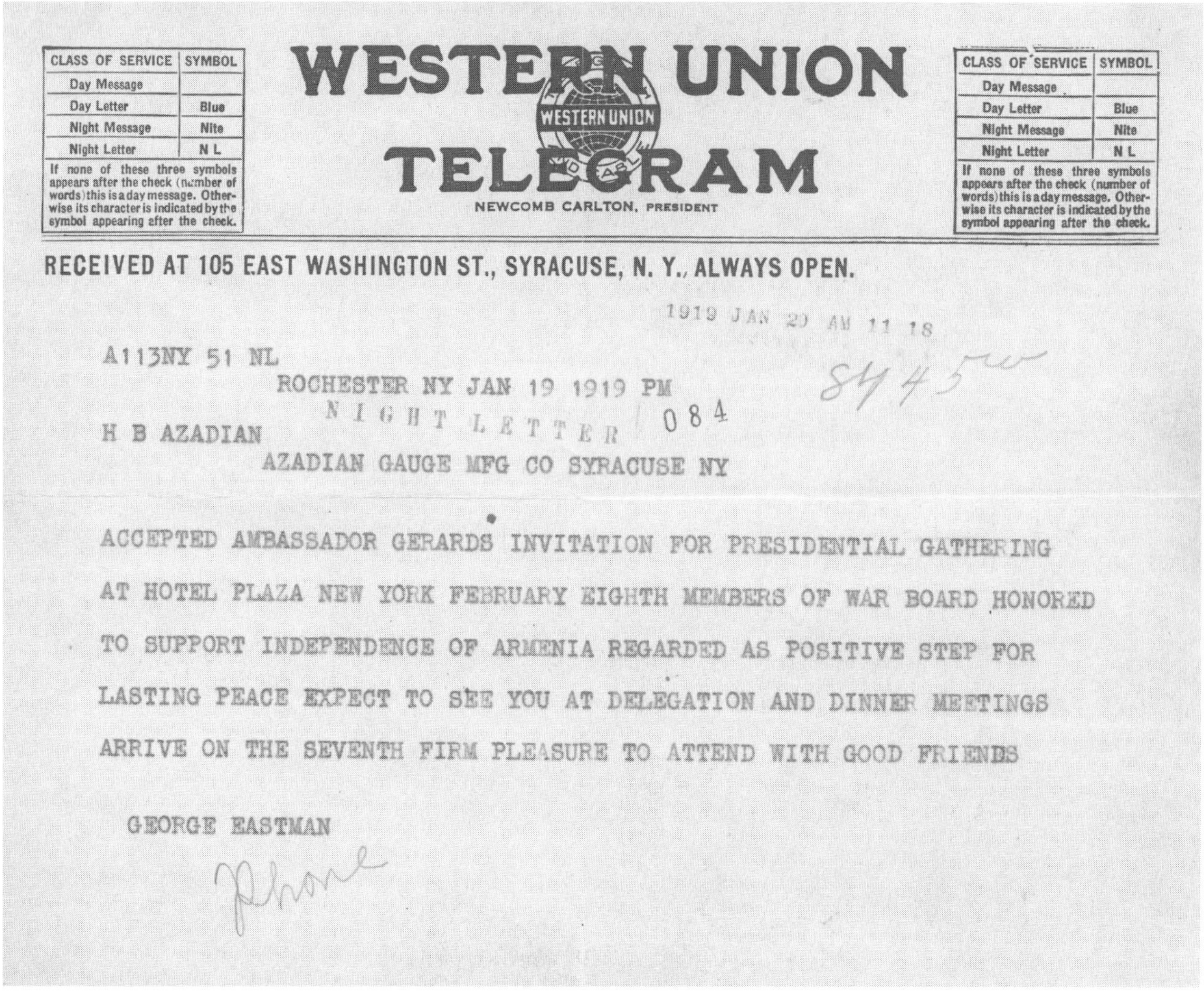

Fig. 54. Telegram from George Eastman to Harutun Azadian, 19 January 1919.

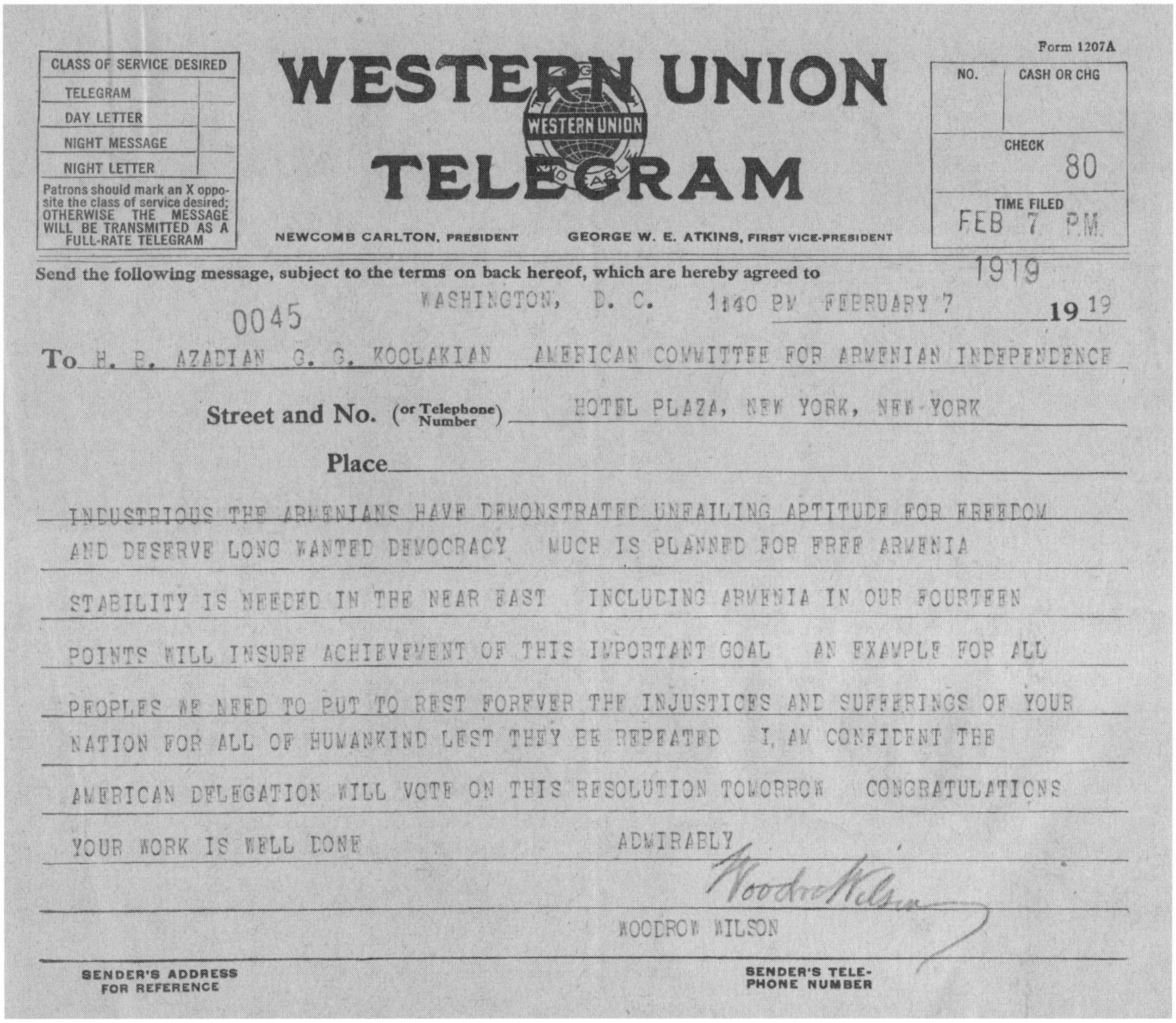

CLASS OF SERVICE DESIRED
TELEGRAM
DAY LETTER
NIGHT MESSAGE
NIGHT LETTER
Patrons should mark an X opposite the class of service desired; OTHERWISE THE MESSAGE WILL BE TRANSMITTED AS A FULL-RATE TELEGRAM

WESTERN UNION TELEGRAM

NEWCOMB CARLTON, PRESIDENT GEORGE W. E. ATKINS, FIRST VICE-PRESIDENT

Form 1207A

NO. CASH OR CHG

CHECK 80

TIME FILED FEB 7 PM

Send the following message, subject to the terms on back hereof, which are hereby agreed to 1919

0045 WASHINGTON, D. C. 1140 PM FEBRUARY 7 1919

To H. B. AZADIAN G. G. KOOLAKIAN AMERICAN COMMITTEE FOR ARMENIAN INDEPENDENCE

Street and No. (or Telephone Number) HOTEL PLAZA, NEW YORK, NEW YORK

Place

INDUSTRIOUS THE ARMENIANS HAVE DEMONSTRATED UNFAILING APTITUDE FOR FREEDOM AND DESERVE LONG WANTED DEMOCRACY MUCH IS PLANNED FOR FREE ARMENIA STABILITY IS NEEDED IN THE NEAR EAST INCLUDING ARMENIA IN OUR FOURTEEN POINTS WILL INSURE ACHIEVEMENT OF THIS IMPORTANT GOAL AN EXAMPLE FOR ALL PEOPLES WE NEED TO PUT TO REST FOREVER THE INJUSTICES AND SUFFERINGS OF YOUR NATION FOR ALL OF HUMANKIND LEST THEY BE REPEATED I AM CONFIDENT THE AMERICAN DELEGATION WILL VOTE ON THIS RESOLUTION TOMORROW CONGRATULATIONS YOUR WORK IS WELL DONE

ADMIRABLY

Woodrow Wilson

WOODROW WILSON

SENDER'S ADDRESS FOR REFERENCE

SENDER'S TELEPHONE NUMBER

Fig. 55. Telegram from Woodrow Wilson to Harutun Azadian and George Koolakian, 7 February 1919.

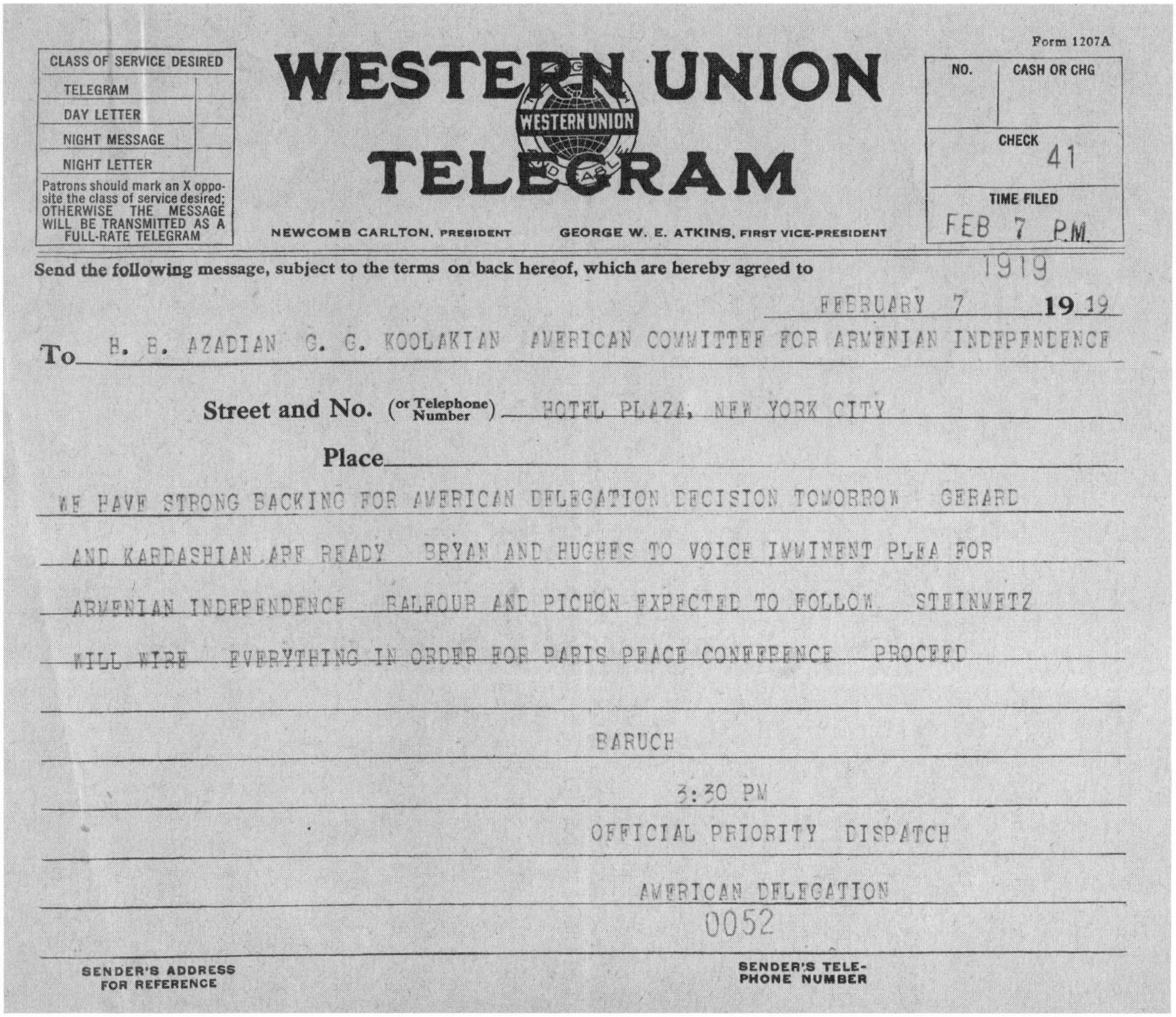

Form 1207A

CLASS OF SERVICE DESIRED
TELEGRAM
DAY LETTER
NIGHT MESSAGE
NIGHT LETTER
Patrons should mark an X opposite the class of service desired; OTHERWISE THE MESSAGE WILL BE TRANSMITTED AS A FULL-RATE TELEGRAM

WESTERN UNION TELEGRAM

NEWCOMB CARLTON, PRESIDENT GEORGE W. E. ATKINS, FIRST VICE-PRESIDENT

NO. CASH OR CHG
CHECK 41
TIME FILED FEB 7 PM. 1919

Send the following message, subject to the terms on back hereof, which are hereby agreed to

FEBRUARY 7 1919

To H. B. AZADIAN G. G. KOOLAKIAN AMERICAN COMMITTEE FOR ARMENIAN INDEPENDENCE

Street and No. (or Telephone Number) HOTEL PLAZA, NEW YORK CITY

Place

WE HAVE STRONG BACKING FOR AMERICAN DELEGATION DECISION TOMORROW GERARD AND KARDASHIAN ARE READY BRYAN AND HUGHES TO VOICE IMMINENT PLEA FOR ARMENIAN INDEPENDENCE BALFOUR AND PICHON EXPECTED TO FOLLOW STEINMETZ WILL WIRE EVERYTHING IN ORDER FOR PARIS PEACE CONFERENCE PROCEED

BARUCH

3:30 PM

OFFICIAL PRIORITY DISPATCH

AMERICAN DELEGATION

0052

SENDER'S ADDRESS FOR REFERENCE

SENDER'S TELEPHONE NUMBER

Fig. 56. Telegram from Bernard M. Baruch to Harutun Azadian and George Koolakian, 7 February 1919.

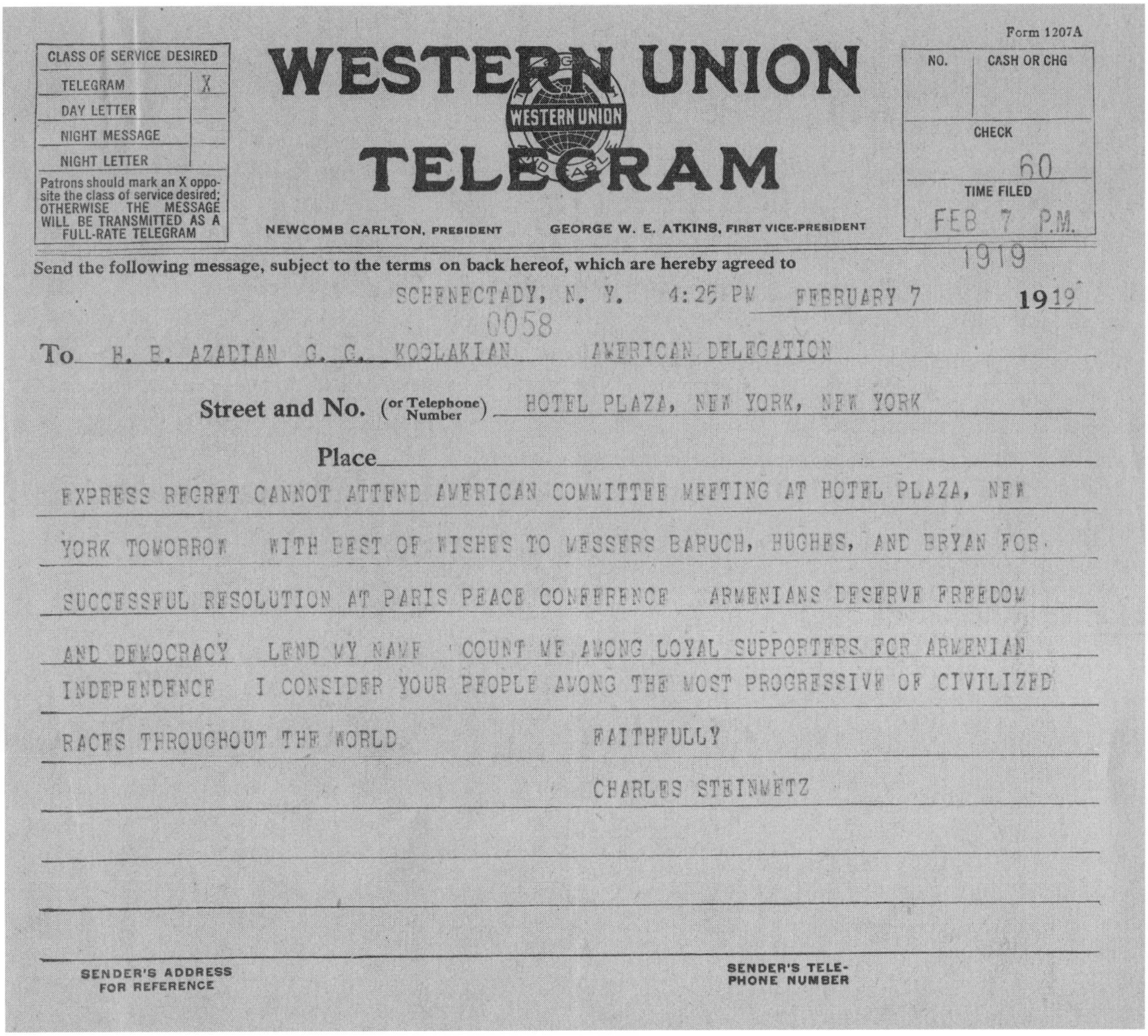

Form 1207A

CLASS OF SERVICE DESIRED	
TELEGRAM	X
DAY LETTER	
NIGHT MESSAGE	
NIGHT LETTER	

Patrons should mark an X opposite the class of service desired; OTHERWISE THE MESSAGE WILL BE TRANSMITTED AS A FULL-RATE TELEGRAM

WESTERN UNION TELEGRAM

NEWCOMB CARLTON, PRESIDENT GEORGE W. E. ATKINS, FIRST VICE-PRESIDENT

NO.	CASH OR CHG
CHECK	60
TIME FILED	FEB 7 P.M. 1919

Send the following message, subject to the terms on back hereof, which are hereby agreed to

SCHENECTADY, N. Y. 4:25 PM FEBRUARY 7 1919

0058

To H. B. AZADIAN G. G. KOOLAKIAN AMERICAN DELEGATION

Street and No. (or Telephone Number) HOTEL PLAZA, NEW YORK, NEW YORK

Place

EXPRESS REGRET CANNOT ATTEND AMERICAN COMMITTEE MEETING AT HOTEL PLAZA, NEW YORK TOMORROW WITH BEST OF WISHES TO MESSERS BARUCH, HUGHES, AND BRYAN FOR SUCCESSFUL RESOLUTION AT PARIS PEACE CONFERENCE ARMENIANS DESERVE FREEDOM AND DEMOCRACY LEND MY NAME COUNT ME AMONG LOYAL SUPPORTERS FOR ARMENIAN INDEPENDENCE I CONSIDER YOUR PEOPLE AMONG THE MOST PROGRESSIVE OF CIVILIZED RACES THROUGHOUT THE WORLD

FAITHFULLY

CHARLES STEINMETZ

SENDER'S ADDRESS FOR REFERENCE

SENDER'S TELEPHONE NUMBER

Fig. 57. Telegram from Charles Steinmetz to Harutun Azadian and George Koolakian, 7 February 1919.

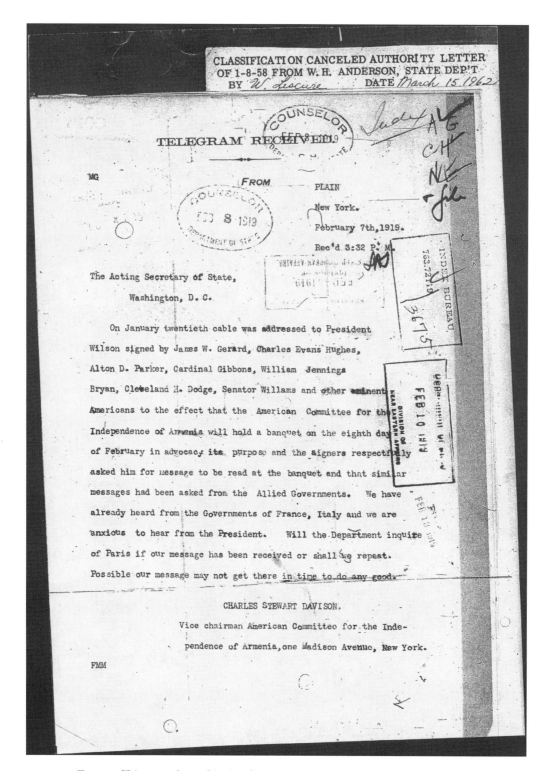

Fig. 58. Telegram from Charles Stewart Davison to the acting secretary of state, 7 February 1919. National Archives and Records Administration, ref. 59.763.72119/3675, United States Department of State Index Bureau file, Counselor Division, Near Eastern Affairs, 7–13 February 1919.

CHAPTER TEN
ALLIED DIGNITARIES GATHER AND ASK, "WHY NOT A REPUBLIC?"

> Our nation has become the mother republic. . . . Our in-
> fluence has reached out until it has touched nation after nation,
> and those nations, rooted in the soil, have become supports of the
> mother tree. . . . Our example has called republics into existence
> throughout Europe; why not a republic in the land where the ark
> rested—the land that gave us the olive branch as the symbol of
> peace.[101]
>
> William Jennings Bryan
> Inaugural Banquet, 8 February 1919

The first official gathering of the American Committee for the Independence of Armenia (ACIA) took place on 8 February 1919, at a banquet in the Grand Ballroom of the Hotel Plaza in New York City (see fig. 59 on page 117).[102] It followed a series of executive committee meetings that began at the hotel on 7 February and continued the next day.[103]

The banquet, which had undergone such intensive preparation in the earliest weeks of 1919, merits some description. Although published accounts vary, we know from documents contained in the Azadian-Koolakian collection that more than four hundred prominent Americans and world figures were present.[104] They included prominent news people; past as well as future United States presidents and their families; state governors; cabinet advisors; House, Senate, and state department representatives; engineers; scientists; educators; actors; composers; recording artists; lawyers; industrialists; financiers; religious leaders; authors; Allied military leaders; noted social reformers; and foreign consular representatives.

Based on the available evidence, a number of guests have been identified. At the head table (see fig. 60 on page 118), from left to right, were (1) Dr. Garegin Pasdermadjian (Armen Garo), *de facto* but not *de jure* ambassador of the Republic of Armenia to the United States; (2) (unknown person); (3) Joseph Tumulty, White House secretary to Woodrow Wilson; (4) Andrew Mellon, financier and future United States treasury secretary; (5) Samson Harutinian, minister of judicial affairs in Armenia's government and member of the Populist Party; (6) Senator Henry Cabot Lodge; (7) Michael Tsamatos, chargé d'affairs of the Greek embassy in Washington, D.C.; (8) Whitney Shepardson, member of the American delegation to the Paris Peace Conference (standing); (9) Louis Loucheur, French delegate to the Paris Peace Conference; (10) Robert S. Brookings, chairman, Price Fixing Committee, United States War Industries Board; (11) Charles Evans Hughes; (12) Ambassador James Gerard, chairman, ACIA; (13) William Jennings Bryan; (14) Bernard M. Baruch (standing), chairman, War Industries Board, and advisor to the American delegation; (15) Gaston Liébert, consul general of France in New York and French delegate to the Paris Peace Conference; (16) Judge Charles McAdoo, Naval War Consulting Board; (17) Baron Nobuaki Makino,[105] foreign minister of Japan and member of the

Supreme Allied Council (or "Council of Ten") at the Paris Peace Conference; (18) Admiral Frank Friday Fletcher, War Industries Board and navy admiral; (19) Arsen Vehouni, formerly head of the Armenian Prelacy in New York[106]; (20) Chonosuke Yada, consul general of Japan; and (21) Admiral Robert Edwin Peary, civil engineer, Naval Consulting Board (of the Peary Expedition fame).

Special and honored NER-ACIA guests were seated at two banquet tables centered directly in front. At the left table were Madeleine Edison Sloane; Carolyn Hawkins (Mrs. Charles) Edison; Mina Miller Edison (Mrs. Thomas A. Edison); James C. McReynolds and William S. Benson, both of the American delegation; and Theda Bara, an early Edison Pioneer and silent motion picture actress. At the second table at the right were Mrs. Corinne Roosevelt Robinson (sister of the former president); the former president's two daughters, Alice Roosevelt Longworth and Ethel Roosevelt; and his widow, Edith Carow Roosevelt.

In the second row, center left, adjacent to the Sloane-Edison party, was table twenty-five with Edith Galt (Mrs. Woodrow) Wilson; William Howard Taft; and Charles J. Bonaparte, former U.S. attorney general (grandnephew of Napoleon Bonaparte). Seated to the right of Bonaparte was Levi Parsons Morton, his longtime friend and associate and America's distinguished political and financial statesman.[107] Seated to the left of Edith Wilson was Manuel Der Manuelian, consul of the Republic of Armenia to the United States. Immediately to the right and adjacent to the Roosevelts, at table twenty-four sat Mr. and Mrs. Harutun and Akabi Azadian, George G. Koolakian, J. Pierpont Morgan Jr., Calvin Coolidge, Grace (Mrs. Calvin) Coolidge, Owen D. Young, and naval secretary Josephus Daniels. At table twenty-six sat Arshalouis ("Aurora") Mardiganian.

In all, five United States presidents and/or their families (past, present, and future) attended the inaugural, accompanied by a majority of American delegation members and advisors to the Paris Peace Conference. Aside from their already recognized strong humanitarian commitment, there was good reason why Americans were devoting so much attention to the Armenian cause.

Not since the Civil War had the United States been involved in such a major conflict. The United States had delayed getting into the war, no doubt hoping to avoid it, in perhaps an unsuccessful last attempt to maintain its isolationism. Reluctantly declaring war against Germany in April 1917 (and against Austria-Hungary in December 1917, but not against Bulgaria and the Ottoman Empire), America went into that conflict in a state of industrial preparedness; it was to emerge at the close of 1918 as a world power. Two years before entering the war, America's reaction to the Turkish atrocities against Armenians and her continued commitment to alleviate the suffering and unfathomable condition of these stricken people had taken many forms in the United States.[108]

Fig. 59. Overview of the banquet, first convention of the American Committee for the Independence of Armenia, Hotel Plaza, New York, Saturday, 8 February 1919.

Fig. 60. View of the banquet head table, first convention of the American Committee for the Independence of Armenia, 8 February 1919.

Immediately following the banquet, the "dinner guests were stirred by a pageant depicting 3,000 years of Armenian history [that] showed some of the trials that Armenia has endured in the cause of civilization and Christianity."[109]

Following the presentations, this was the order of the proceedings:

> James W. Gerard, chairman [of the ACIA] who presided, asserted that the claims of Armenia could not be ignored by the [Paris] peace conference. He told of the hundreds of thousands of Armenians slaughtered by the Turks because the Armenian people refused to support Turkey in Turkey's support of Kultur. He [then] paid a tribute to the heroism of the Armenian contingent that fought with the Allies in Palestine. Armenia has earned freedom, he said.
>
> Then, "[a] resolution was passed [by members of the American delegation present] asking the [Paris] peace conference to help Armenia to establish an independent state," and "the Armenian National Delegation at Paris sent an expression of thanks for America's interest in Armenian freedom."[110]
>
> "Messages from Foreign Minister Balfour of England and Foreign Minister Pichon of France, promising the support of those nations to the cause of Armenian independence, were received with applause" as "James W. Gerard . . . read the message from Balfour and Gaston Liebert, French Consul General, read the cable from Pichon."[111]

Amid those acknowledgments, "Charles Evans Hughes and William Jennings Bryan made pleas for a free Armenia." Speaking in the spirit of the time, "Mr. Bryan recounted the achievements of the United States in popular government. . . . The nation, he declared, was an example and in a position to be a teacher to the democracies of the world, its policies having been vindicated by the victory over autocracy and its virility and progress being testified to."[112] The silver-tongued orator continued in this fashion:

> It is appropriate . . . that the Armenians, some 100,000 in numbers, who have come to this country should be our ambassadors to carry not only our greeting but our ideals to their brethren in Armenia.[113] Let them relate to the martyrs of Armenia the thrilling story of our nation's life and progress; let them tell how we build securely upon the solid foundation of a people's consent; how completely we trust the intelligence, the integrity and the patriotism of our citizens; how every step has been a step forward toward more popular methods of government. Let them proclaim the value of free speech and of a free press built upon the theory of Jefferson that "error is harmless when reason is left free to combat it." . . .

We have always been the friends of the Armenians, admiring their industry, their intellectual alertness, their keenness, their sobriety, their aptitude for education and affairs, and we have revolted at the thought of such a people being under the yoke of the Turk.

Now, we rejoice that the hour of liberation has come. The vain ambition of brute force has overreached itself and has resulted in the emancipation of the downtrodden and oppressed of centuries. . . .

There is no doubt of the capacity of the Armenians for freedom. They have shown a racial solidarity and a capacity to survive incredible misfortunes; they have rare intelligence, and no people prize more highly the advantages of education.

All they need is a fair opportunity, that decent opportunity which only civil and religious liberty can provide. . . .

We propose to-night to throw such influence as we have into the scale for Armenian independence. It would be unthinkable that Armenia should be left longer under Turkish control, and if it is not under Turkish control then Armenia should be autonomous. We see no insurmountable obstacle to the attainment of this happy result. We believe that under Armenian control those sections of country which constitute Armenia can be well governed with proper regard for the just rights of all within their borders.

In saying this with all my heart, I do not wish to be understood as favoring any proposal that the United States should undertake a protectorate of Armenia. I do not believe that such a proposal would be wise. It is not necessary. It is no more necessary that America should assume a virtual protectorate of Armenia than that Great Britain or France should assume a protectorate of Cuba.

We do, however, desire that our just influence, exerted in any proper way, shall be thrown on the side of the independence of Armenia. We are peculiarly sensitive to her appeal and we desire for her the prosperous future to which the industry and genius of her people entitle her.[114]

During the program, toastmaster James W. Gerard acknowledged special and honored guests. Tributes were given to the late President Theodore Roosevelt and to members of the Roosevelt family who attended on his behalf. A posthumous recognition was also given to the late Julia Ward Howe with an overview of Mrs. Howe's lengthy commitment to the ABCFM and to the Armenian cause.[115] The legacy of her time-honored commitment lived on among her colleagues and friends who came to partake in that candlelit hall in the spirit of justice and humanity now being addressed by the participants who assembled there. All of them came to speak on behalf of Armenian independence that evening, to right human injustices by exemplifying the plight of the Armenian people as the compassionate Woodrow Wilson so astutely observed:

"to put to rest forever the injustices and sufferings of [Armenia] for all of humankind lest they be repeated."[116]

Then the prominent New York City Armenian lawyer-historian M. Vartan Malcom (seated at table twenty-three) delivered a message to the ACIA convention:

> The Armenians claim the absolute independence of their country on the ground that they are lawfully entitled to sovereign possession of their native land just as much as Frenchmen are to France and Englishmen are to England; and all they ask for is their own country. Moreover, the Allies have under various treaties, not only recognized the justice of her claim but also promised to liberate her from Turkey, although they failed to carry out these solemn covenants. Furthermore, in the beginning of the recent war, the Armenians found themselves between Russia and Turkey, but they bravely joined the side of right and justice and fought as co-belligerents with the Allies. They thus sacrificed over 25 per cent of their entire population while the losses of France are said to be less than 5 or 6 per cent. No nation on either side of the war, including Belgium, Servia and Roumania, has suffered more, contributed more and shed more blood for freedom than the Armenians. And they are to-day demanding that the Great Powers shall not again make a pawn of their country, but restore it to its lawful owners and declare its complete Independence in the forthcoming Treaty.[117]

Although no formal document is known to exist that details the exact sequence of events on that occasion, a 22 January 1919 memorandum from Charles V. Vickrey to the ACIA Banquet Planning Committee provides probably the most reliable source of information about how that historic weekend event had been planned by officials of the ABCFM and the ACASR/NER. On 22 January, certain decisions had been made:

> It is the consensus of the American Committee that posthumous recognitions shall be bestowed to the late President Theodore Roosevelt and to Mrs. Julia Ward Howe, in that order, followed by a moment of silence.
>
> The Roosevelts will command the place of honor in front of the speaker's podium head table.
>
> At the moment guests are assembled, the meeting will be called to order by Ambassador Gerard, presiding. Electric illumination will be dimmed throughout the great hall and then extinguished as the candle sconces are lighted, beginning with the Roosevelts. The lighting will then proceed to the head table, then follow in sequence, row by row, across the hall to the rear until the entire forum is illuminated in soft candlelight.

Ambassador Gerard, presiding, shall bestow the recognition to Mrs. Roosevelt, or if she is not present, to Mrs. Alice Roosevelt Longworth, the late president's eldest daughter.

Posthumous recognition for Armenian Relief shall then follow in honor of the late Mrs. Julia Ward Howe, to be received by Dr. James L. Barton of the American Board of Commissioners.

Mme. Yvonne De Treville will sing the "Battle Hymn of the Republic" with musical accompaniment. She will then sing "Armenia" a new musical arrangement by Claude Warford, prepared for the ceremony.

Invocation will follow, administered by the Very Reverend Arsene Vehouni, Armenian Archbishop.

Dinner to be served—

Conclusion of the dinner, electric illumination will be restored.

Serving of dessert will signal Ambassador Gerard's introduction of the head table. Mr. Gerard will recognize other special guests and honored citizens, and will acknowledge opening messages.

Ambassador Gerard shall recognize Mrs. George Vanderbilt and Mrs. Oliver Harriman, who will present background for the Armenian Pageant. They will also introduce the American Committee guest of the evening, Miss Arshalouis Mardiganian, explaining her autobiography "Armenia Ravished" and her role in translating that autobiography into the motion picture for the cause of Armenian Relief. The National Motion Picture Association will also recognize Mr. George Eastman for his contributions to the filming and mastering of this production on behalf of Armenian and Syrian Relief.

Ambassador Gerard will address the floor, introducing the guest speakers, the Honorable Charles Evans Hughes, and the Honorable William Jennings Bryan. Unless otherwise noted, they will address the banquet in that order.

Mr. Gerard will acknowledge later cables and other messages following the guest speakers.

Ambassador Gerard will introduce Mr. Bernard Baruch of the American Delegation.

Mr. Baruch will address the American Delegates, requesting them to introduce to the floor a resolution for the provision of Armenian independence. They will cast their votes to petition the International Peace Conference. Their decision will be wire cabled to Paris directly from the floor of the Plaza.

Acknowledgement of late messages and closing statements by Ambassador Gerard.

Presentation of the Armenian National Anthem "Mer Haiasdan" (Our Armenia) a duette with accompaniment performed by Miss Lucine Paragian and Phillip Bennyan.

Benediction

Later meetings to be announced for the week of February 9th.

C.V.V. [Charles V. Vickrey]
January 22, 1919[118]

The 8 February 1919 inaugural gathering of the ACIA was the first time in American history that so many groups came together to support a common cause for justice on behalf of a minority people in spite of their differing political and professional backgrounds. Armenian sympathies in the United States were at an all-time high at the close of World War I, having permeated almost every aspect of the American experience.

Following the inaugural, Azadian and Koolakian remained in New York through Tuesday morning, 11 February, attending informal gatherings with the American Committee and the NER. Although they were never outwardly vocal over their achievements, the Azadians and Koolakians must have shared a deep sense of satisfaction when they read the newspaper accounts of the event. They dined that Sunday afternoon sharing this information in quiet celebration of Mr. and Mrs. Azadian's eighteenth wedding anniversary.

Returning to Syracuse early in the evening of Tuesday, 11 February, Azadian and Koolakian went home to their respective families and prepared for the shortened work week ahead.[119] Woodrow Wilson would soon return to the United States from his lengthy first session at the Paris Peace Conference. He did not yet know the exact course his Fourteen Points and League of Nations would take during later peace conference negotiations, although he still had an expectation of Armenian independence. On 26 February, soon after returning to the United States, President Wilson wired Azadian and Koolakian (see fig. 61 on page 126).

Pressing on, Wilson soon returned to Paris to address later sessions of the peace conference. However, it was evident by June that he had been pressured by the Allied Powers to accept certain compromises in his Fourteen Points in exchange for their acceptance of the covenant forming the League of Nations as a basis for ratification of the peace treaty. Returning to the United States later that month, President Wilson found that the Senate was not yet reconciled:

> [The Senate was] bitterly opposed to ratification of the Treaty [of peace with Germany, which would establish the League of Nations] unless certain [other] concessions were made. Wilson was equally adamant in refusing to make concessions. Confident that once the [American] people understood the issues they would support him, he set forth in September 1919 on a speaking tour of the country, hoping to convince the voters that the treaty should be ratified and that a league of nations should be established. Before the end of the month he collapsed from fatigue and was forced to return to Washington. There he suffered a paralytic stroke which

made him an invalid for the remaining eighteen months of his term of office.[120]

It was under these conditions that Armenia, once a fundamental part of President Wilson's Fourteen Points and the peace settlement, soon found itself mired amid mounting political controversy with other aspects of the international proposal. This controversy would forestall the ratification of a peace treaty by the United States for several years and was to derail the Armenian independence movement in America, which underwent intense political fragmentation among prominent members of the Armenian American community.

For Azadian and Koolakian, moved primarily by humanitarian impulses, it became evident by the middle of 1920 that little was to be accomplished by the well-intentioned Armenian independence movement in America. Devoid of political ambition and with a decided dislike for political controversy, they would withdraw as liaisons. The end for them seems to have been clinched while preparations were under way for a mass meeting of the ACIA in New York on 30 May 1920, the second anniversary observance of Armenia's self-declared independence. A few days before that meeting took place, an urgent message dated 27 May was communicated to Azadian from the Armenian National Democratic Party, instructing them to take no part in the meeting. It seems that a faction of influential Armenians was urging certain United States senators to oppose an American mandate of Armenia, thus dealing a blow to the Armenian cause (see fig. 62 on page 127).

Furthermore, a major disagreement in the United States over the adoption of the League of Nations covenant was now having a resounding effect on the Armenian independence movement in America, impacting the Armenian American community in a way that would color it for the next three-quarters of a century.

By the close of 1920, the fate of the first short-lived Armenian independence movement was revealed to the Western world. Little protection was given to Armenia's fledgling democracy against the advancing armies of Turkey's new military leader, Mustafa Kemal (later Atatürk), which inflicted heavy losses on the resident population and those who had sought refuge in those lands. To save itself, the remaining portion of the Armenian republic surrendered to the advancing Red Army. Armenia was sovietized in December 1920.

Had the plight of Armenia been forgotten? Were the pleas and promises of that impressive first Armenian independence convention heard no more? Many Armenian Americans and their supporters felt the deepest sense of disappointment, if not betrayal. Although Azadian and Koolakian had had deep hopes for a democratically free and independent Armenia, nothing could assuage the devastating losses the Armenian massacres had wrought on their immediate families. Talking little of those circumstances, they lived out the remainder of their lives ever grateful to have shared the American experience, hoping, no doubt, that Armenia's opportunity for independence would finally come one day.

The Swiss historian Elisabeth Bauer made this fitting assessment of the Turkish depredations on the Armenian people:

The Turks treated the unarmed Christian population with inconceivable cruelty when the outbreak of the First World War gave them the opportunity to carry out their fateful internal policies. Spurred on by foreign interest in the plan of annihilating the Armenians and annexing their territory, the Turks robbed themselves of their most valuable citizens. Only the Armenians were capable of saving this "Sick Man of Europe" from its fanatic, religiously inspired opposition to progress, of curing its economy, educating its youth and developing in its people an appreciation of order and work. The calculation of the Turkish authorities that none of the Christian peoples would intercede for their co-religionists proved correct. The shocking evidence (photographs, diplomatic correspondence, and the reports of Swiss and of American Missionaries) revealed to the world that more had begun in Anatolia than just the first genocide of the twentieth century; the people of the first Christian nation in the world were following a via dolorosa like that of the founder of their religion, undergoing a martyrdom for the sake of their spirits and their culture which could have repercussions throughout Christendom [and the World]. An impartial history demands the expiation of these crimes against humanity so that a new beginning can be made, unburdened by the past.[121]

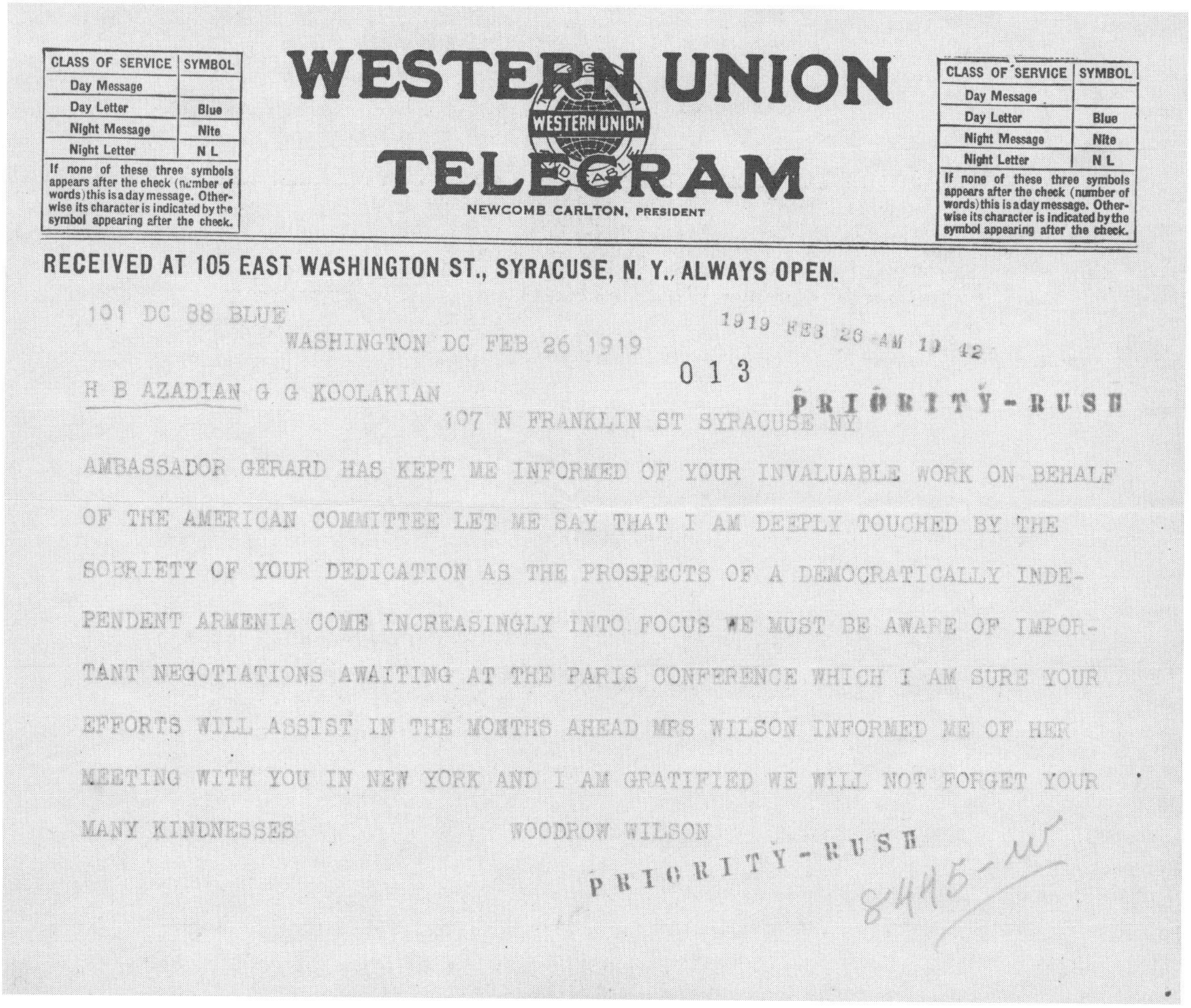

WESTERN UNION
TELEGRAM
NEWCOMB CARLTON, PRESIDENT

CLASS OF SERVICE | SYMBOL
Day Message |
Day Letter | Blue
Night Message | Nite
Night Letter | N L
If none of these three symbols appears after the check (number of words) this is a day message. Otherwise its character is indicated by the symbol appearing after the check.

CLASS OF SERVICE | SYMBOL
Day Message |
Day Letter | Blue
Night Message | Nite
Night Letter | N L
If none of these three symbols appears after the check (number of words) this is a day message. Otherwise its character is indicated by the symbol appearing after the check.

RECEIVED AT 105 EAST WASHINGTON ST., SYRACUSE, N. Y., ALWAYS OPEN.

101 DC 88 BLUE

WASHINGTON DC FEB 26 1919   1919 FEB 26 AM 10 42

013

H B AZADIAN G G KOOLAKIAN   PRIORITY-RUSH

107 N FRANKLIN ST SYRACUSE NY

AMBASSADOR GERARD HAS KEPT ME INFORMED OF YOUR INVALUABLE WORK ON BEHALF

OF THE AMERICAN COMMITTEE LET ME SAY THAT I AM DEEPLY TOUCHED BY THE

SOBRIETY OF YOUR DEDICATION AS THE PROSPECTS OF A DEMOCRATICALLY INDE-

PENDENT ARMENIA COME INCREASINGLY INTO FOCUS WE MUST BE AWARE OF IMPOR-

TANT NEGOTIATIONS AWAITING AT THE PARIS CONFERENCE WHICH I AM SURE YOUR

EFFORTS WILL ASSIST IN THE MONTHS AHEAD MRS WILSON INFORMED ME OF HER

MEETING WITH YOU IN NEW YORK AND I AM GRATIFIED WE WILL NOT FORGET YOUR

MANY KINDNESSES   WOODROW WILSON

PRIORITY-RUSH

Fig. 61. Telegram from Woodrow Wilson to Harutun Azadian and George Koolakian, 26 February 1919.

WESTERN UNION TELEGRAM

Form 1201

CLASS OF SERVICE	SYMBOL
Telegram	
Day Letter	Blue
Night Message	Nite
Night Letter	N L

If none of these three symbols appears after the check (number of words) this is a telegram. Otherwise its character is indicated by the symbol appearing after the check.

NEWCOMB CARLTON, PRESIDENT   GEORGE W. E. ATKINS, FIRST VICE-PRESIDENT

CLASS OF SERVICE	SYMBOL
Telegram	
Day Letter	Blue
Night Message	Nite
Night Letter	N L

If none of these three symbols appears after the check (number of words) this is a telegram. Otherwise its character is indicated by the symbol appearing after the check.

RECEIVED AT

18B RU 85 NLNL 2 EX NL

BOSTON MASS MAY 27 1920

G A AGHAIAN   0036

735 EAST WASHINGTON ST SYRACUSE NY

IT IS RECENTLY DISCLOSED IN WASHINGTON THAT ACCORDING TO AUTHORITATIVE

STATEMENT PASDERMAJIAN BISHOP MURATBEGIAN AND KARDASHIAN HAVE JOINTLY

APPEALED TO LODGE SPENCER HARDING AND OTHER INFLUENTIAL SENATORS EXPRES

-SING OPPOSITION TO AMERICAN MENDATE   OF ARMENIA THIS IS THE HARDEST BLOW

OUR NATIONAL CAUSE HAS EVER SUFFERED OWING TO AND IN PROTEST OF THIS

TREACHEROUS ACTION ON THE PART OF PASDERMAJIAN CLIC WE DECIDED WITH DRAWAL

FROM PARTICIPATION IN THE SECOND ANNIVERSARY CELEBRATION SUNDAY WE

INSTRUCT YOU NOT TO TAKE ANY PART IN THE MASS MEETING

CENTRAL COMMITTEE OF ARMENIAN   NATIONAL DEMOCRATIC PARTY
DIKIJIAN ANA   630 A   MAY 28

Fig. 62. Telegram from Ana [Iacuna] Dikijian of the Central Committee of the Armenian National Democratic Party to G. A. Aghaian, 27 May 1920.

64TH CONGRESS,
1ST SESSION. **S. CON. RES. 12.**

IN THE SENATE OF THE UNITED STATES.

FEBRUARY 9, 1916.

Mr. LODGE submitted the following concurrent resolution; which was considered and agreed to.

CONCURRENT RESOLUTION.

Whereas in countries now engaged in war there are several hundreds of thousands of Armenians in need of food, clothing, and shelter; and

Whereas great numbers of them have been required by conditions growing out of the state of war to leave their homes and their property, deprived of an opportunity to make provision for their most elementary wants, causing starvation, disease, and untold suffering; and

Whereas the people of the United States of America have learned with sorrow of this terrible plight of great numbers of human beings and have most generously responded to the cry for help whenever such an appeal has reached them: Therefore be it

1   *Resolved by the Senate (the House of Representatives*
2   *concurring),* That, in view of the misery, wretchedness,
3   and hardships which these people are suffering, the Presi-
4   dent of the United States be respectfully asked to desig-
5   nate a day on which the citizens of this country may give

2

1   nate a day on which the citizens of this country may give
2   expression to their sympathy by contributing to the funds
3   now being raised for the relief of the Armenians in the
4   belligerent countries.

Passed the Senate February 9, 1916.

Attest: JAMES M. BAKER,

Secretary.

64TH CONGRESS,) **S. CON. RES. 12.**
1ST SESSION.)

[Report No. 887.]

CONCURRENT RESOLUTION

Requesting the President of the United States to designate a day on which funds may be raised for the relief of the Armenians

FEBRUARY 10, 1916.—Referred to the Committee on Foreign Affairs.

JUNE 21, 1916.—Referred to the House Calendar and ordered to be printed.

The text of Senate Congressional Resolution 12, designating a day for raising funds for the relief of Armenians, passed 9 February 1916.

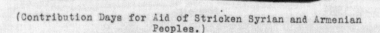

(Contribution Days for Aid of Stricken Syrian and Armenian
Peoples.)

By the President of the United States of America.

A PROCLAMATION.

WHEREAS, I have received from the Senate of the

United States a Resolution, passed July 7 (calendar day,

July 10), 1916, reading as follows:

"Whereas the attention of the people of
the United States has been directed to the helpless situation in which many of the Syrians in
the Mount Lebanon district have been placed, and
that many thousands have perished from hunger
and exposure; and

"Whereas thousands of citizens of the United
States in practically every State of the Union
were either born in Syria or are the children of
Syrians born in that country, and that thousands
of American citizens are related by blood and
affinity to many of the said suffering and helpless people; and

"Whereas the people of the United States have
demonstrated their sympathy for the suffering
people on all sides in the great European war,
having helped in a practical way the people of
Belgium, Serbia, Ireland, Poland, and others, as
becomes a nation which is neutral in this war and
on friendly terms with all the belligerents:
Therefore be it

"Resolved, That, appreciating the sufferings
of the Syrian people, it is suggested that the
President of the United States set aside a day upon
which a direct appeal to the sympathy of all American citizens shall be made and an opportunity shall
be given for our public-spirited people to contribute to a much-needed fund for the relief of the
Syrian people."

And Whereas, a Resolution was passed by the Congress

of the United States on July 18, 1916, reading as follows:

"Whereas in countries now engaged in war there
are several hundreds of thousands of Armenians in
need of food, clothing, and shelter; and

"Whereas great numbers of them have been required by conditions growing out of the state of
war to leave their homes and their property, deprived of an opportunity to make provision for
their most elementary wants, causing starvation,

disease,

Presidential Proclamation 1345, "Contribution Days for Aid of Stricken Syrian and Armenian Peoples," proclaiming Saturday, 21 October, and Sunday, 22 October, of 1916 as days in which the people of the United States may make contributions "for the aid of the stricken Syrian and Armenian peoples."

disease, and untold suffering; and

"Whereas the people of the United States
of America have learned with sorrow of this
terrible plight of great numbers of human beings
and have most generously responded to the cry
for help whenever such an appeal has reached
them: Therefore be it

"Resolved by the Senate (the House of Representatives concurring), That, in view of the misery,
wretchedness, and hardships which these people are
suffering, the President of the United States be
respectfully asked to designate a day on which the
citizens of this country may give expression to
their sympathy by contributing to the funds now
being raised for the relief of the Armenians in
the belligerent countries."

And Whereas, I feel confident that the people of the

United States will be moved to aid these peoples stricken

by war, famine and disease;

Now, therefore, I, Woodrow Wilson, President of the

United States, in compliance with the said suggestion of the

Senate, and the said request of the Congress thereof; do

appoint and proclaim Saturday, October 21, and Sunday,

October 22, 1916, as joint days upon which the people of

the United States may make such contributions as they feel

disposed for the aid of the stricken Syrian and Armenian

peoples.

Contributions may be addressed to the American Red

Cross, Washington, D. C., which will care for their proper

distribution.

In Witness Whereof, I have hereunto set my hand

and caused the seal of the United States to be affixed.

Done

1345

Page two of Presidential Proclamation 1345, "Contribution Days for Aid of Stricken Syrian and Armenian Peoples," proclaiming Saturday, 21 October, and Sunday, 22 October, of 1916 as days in which the people of the United States may make contributions "for the aid of the stricken Syrian and Armenian peoples."

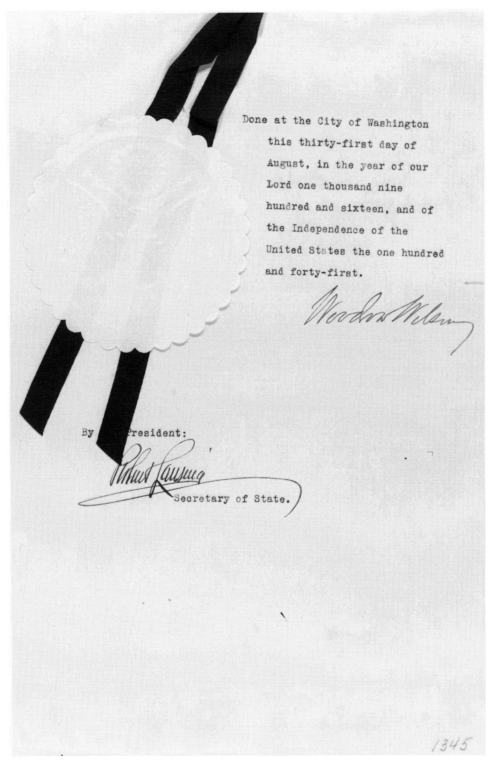

Done at the City of Washington
this thirty-first day of
August, in the year of our
Lord one thousand nine
hundred and sixteen, and of
the Independence of the
United States the one hundred
and forty-first.

Woodrow Wilson

By the President:

Robert Lansing
Secretary of State.

1345

Page three of Presidential Proclamation 1345, "Contribution Days for Aid of Stricken Syrian and Armenian Peoples," proclaiming Saturday, 21 October, and Sunday, 22 October, of 1916 as days in which the people of the United States may make contributions "for the aid of the stricken Syrian and Armenian peoples."

1. United States Department of State documents sometimes refer to the organization as the American Committee for Armenian Independence or the American Commission for Armenian Independence.

2. At that time, the Plaza Hotel was also called the Hotel Plaza.

3. Joseph L. Grabill, *Protestant Diplomacy and the Near East: Missionary Influence on American Foreign Policy, 1810–1927* (Minneapolis: University of Minnesota Press, 1971), 5.

4. *Near East Relief, 1915–1990* (New York: Near East Foundation, 1990), 5, 6, 7.

5. Grabill, *Protestant Diplomacy.*

6. *Papers Relating to the Foreign Relations of the United States with the Annual Message of the President Transmitted to Congress, December 2, 1895, Part II* (Washington, D.C.: Government Printing Office, 1896), 1232–1473.

7. The United States did not have formal ambassadors until 1893, with the appointment of ambassadors to Great Britain and France (see the Secretary of State Web site, Office of the Historian, Frequently Asked Questions, http://www.state.gov/r/pa/ho/faq/). Not until 1906 did the United States appoint an ambassador to the Ottoman Empire (see http://www.state.gov/r/pa/ho/po/com/11324.htm).

8. *Papers Relating to the Foreign Relations of the United States . . . 1895, Part II,* 1392.

9. Ibid., 1393.

10. William E. Barton, *The Life of Clara Barton* (New York: AMS Press, 1969), 2:244.

11. E. A. Brayley Hodgetts, *Round about Armenia: The Record of a Journey across the Balkans through Turkey, the Caucasus, and Persia in 1895* (London: Sampson Low, Marston and Company, 1896), 4.

12. Marion Harland, *Under the Flag of the Orient* (Philadelphia: Historical Publishing Company, 1897), 415.

13. Cyrus Hamlin, quoted in Alice Stone Blackwell, *Armenian Poems Rendered into English Verse* (Boston: Robert Chambers, 1917), x.

14. Edwin Augustus Grosvenor, *Constantinople* (Boston: Roberts Brothers, 1895), 1:102, quoted in Vatche Ghazarian, ed., *Armenians in the Ottoman Empire:*

An Anthology of Transformation, 13th–19th Centuries (Waltham, Mass.: Mayreni Publishing, 1997), 647.

15. Blackwell, *Armenian Poems*, iii.

16. Ibid., 91.

17. Edwin Pears, *Turkey and Its People* (London: Methuen and Co., 1911), 270.

18. James L. Barton, an American of English heritage, called the Armenians "the Anglo-Saxons of Eastern Turkey"; the Frenchman Alphonse de Lamartine, who fled to Switzerland during the Napoleonic Wars, called the Armenians "the Swiss of the Near East"; and the American Samuel Sullivan Cox wrote that the Armenians were the "Yankees of the Orient." This was quoted in Blackwell, *Armenian Poems*, viii and ix, and in Ghazarian, *Armenians in the Ottoman Empire*, 613, respectively.

19. Alice Stone Blackwell, in the introduction to her *Armenian Poems* (1917), commented that "Armenia was the seat of one of the most ancient civilizations of the globe. Its people were contemporary with the Assyrians and Babylonians. They are of Aryan race, and of pure Caucasian blood. Their origin is lost in the mists of antiquity. According to their own tradition, they are the descendants of Thorkom, or Togarmah, a grandson of Japhet, who settled in Armenia after the Ark rested on Ararat. They call themselves Haik, and their country Haiasdan, after Haig, the son of Togarmah, one of their greatest kings." The origins of the Armenian people are discussed in detail by British historian David Marshall Lang in his *Armenia: Cradle of Civilization* (London: George, Allen and Unwin, 1970), 78–83.

20. Harry V. Osborne, "The Near East and World Peace: A Discourse Prepared for the Honorable Woodrow Wilson, President of the United States" (unpublished manuscript) (Boston: ABCFM, 1913), 1–7. This discourse included seven articles over twenty-three pages: (1) "Important Features of the Near Eastern Question," (2) "An Autonomous Armenia-Syria," (3) "The Possible Settlement—A Federation of the Near East," (4) "Why the Turk Must Not Dominate in Turkey," (5) "The Triple Alliance—Germany, Italy, Austria, Hungary," (6) "The Triple Entente—France, Russia, England," and (7) "The Prospects of the Federation—World Peace." Osborne later became a member of the National Committee of the ACASR/NER upon its organization late in 1915. Although little credited, his work was important in anticipating the formation of the ACIA at the end of World War I. This series of articles was prepared by the ABCFM for submission to President Wilson in 1913; however, no evidence of it has been found to date in the sixty-nine volumes of *The Papers of Woodrow Wilson*, Arthur S. Link, ed. (Princeton: Princeton University Press, 1966–94).

21. Osborne, "The Near East," 5.

22. Herbert Hoover, *The Memoirs of Herbert Hoover: Years of Adventure, 1874–1920* (New York: Macmillan, 1951), v–vi, 385.

23. Although Near East Relief was not officially incorporated by Congressional proclamation until 6 August 1919, it is evident that the ACASR was already being informally recognized by the new name at least seven months prior to that event.

24. Excerpt from the official proclamation signed by Woodrow Wilson, 31 August 1916, establishing 21 and 22 October 1916 as days of relief observance for the Armenians, based upon Senate Concurrent Resolution No. 12 approved by the United States Congress on 18 July 1916. This annual observance beginning in 1916 became popularly known as President Wilson's Armenian-Syrian Relief Days. Inexplicably, this proclamation is not in *The Papers of Woodrow Wilson,* but its existence is verified in a memorandum from Charles V. Vickrey, executive secretary of the ACASR in New York, to Syracuse coworkers, 21 October 1916. See Appendices 1 and 2 on pages 129, 130, 131, and 132 for the texts of the Senate resolution and of Proclamation 1345.

25. Bryce is possibly referring to President Wilson's 22 January 1917 Senate address.

26. Link, *Papers of Woodrow Wilson,* 41:217.

27. "Address to the Nation at Kansas City, September 6, 1919," in Link, *Papers of Woodrow Wilson,* 63:71.

28. "Address to the Nation at Salt Lake City, September 23, 1919," in Link, *Papers of Woodrow Wilson,* 63:458.

29. Link, *Papers of Woodrow Wilson,* 53:180.

30. Ibid.

31. This was probably filed by way of the Swedish legation, since the United States, from 20 April 1917 on, had no diplomatic relations with the Ottoman Empire. Koolakian eventually received the visas in 1920 through the British high commissioner's office in Constantinople.

32. James Empringham, *The Story of a God-Fearing People,* from *Armenia, "A Christian Nation": Her Heart-Rending Cry,* 3 (printed broadside of the Syracuse Fund a Committee for Relief in Armenia, undated, but contains time-specific NER information placing its first printing in December 1915).

33. The districts are set down in great detail in a *Map of the Mission of the ABCFM in Western Turkey* (Boston: ABCFM, 1880) with descriptive legend (A. Meisel and Co., Lithographers) in the papers of Harutun Azadian and George

Koolakian, hereafter cited as Azadian-Koolakian Papers.

34. William W. Peet Jr. to Mrs. H. B. Azadian, 9 November 1915 through 21 December 1949 (fragmented), Azadian-Koolakian Papers.

35. William W. Peet Sr. to Mrs. H. B. Azadian; also correspondence files, William W. Peet Sr. (hereafter William Peet), the ABCFM, and Mrs. W. W. Peet, et al.; Johanna Zimmer, 28 September 1892 to 8 March 1918; also roster and photograph of Armenian orphan girls, ABCFM school, Constantinople, 1896 (fragmented), Azadian-Koolakian Papers.

36. Alice Stone Blackwell to Mrs. H. B. Azadian, 12 April 1908, Azadian-Koolakian Papers.

37. Among Azadian's papers are original engravings and proof strikings that were executed by "Artemy (Harutun) Azadian" under the established trade name "Ivanovitsch Zaduni," or "I Z," both employing the ancient "Arata" or Urartian, form of the A'Zad(ian) surname in the 1840s, 1850s, and 1860s. Ivanovitsch's business and family relationships are described in three investigative probate papers written in 1907 in German by Adolf Dattan (a friend of the Azadians), a vice consul of the German Empire:
    1. "Erbansprueche von Artin Mardiros Azadian an den Nachlas von Mardiros Artjemeff (Artenjen)," Naumburg, Germany, July 1907.
    2. "Eingesandten Papieren Ersichtlich auch das Nicolai Artjemeff (Artenjen) am 6ten Juli, 1883 in Baku ermordet wurde die Schulden Hinterliess die seitens des Mardiros Artin Artjemeff (Artenjen) Erbe anerkannt aber wegen noch zu Erbschaftmasse, Adolf Dattan am 6ten Juli, 1907."
    3. "Uebersetzung Auszug Aus den Civilgesetzen des Russischen Kaiserreiches" (legal supplement) July 1907.
Russian equivalents were similarly researched and filed in Odessa by Adolf Dattan's colleague Ernst Fedorovitsch von Kappenberg, a civil attorney who was investigating Azadian family holdings within the Russian Empire.

38. Adolf Dattan records, and also confirmed by engravings among the Azadian papers.

39. Ibid.

40. Many of these early affiliations and travels are verified in the correspondence of Adolf Dattan, dated 25 July, written to "Artin Mardiros Azadian" regarding the Last Will and Testament of "Nicolai Artjemeff Artenjen" (deceased 6 July 1883) under legal probate "5 September 1885 in Baku" according to "Frist von 5 Jahren erfolgen koenne . . . des Bakuer Gouverneurs ausgefertigt, dass Mardiros Artjemeff" (Mardiros Azadian). Also corroborated in E. Bénézit, *Dictionnaire critique et documentaire des peintres, sculpteurs, dessinateurs et graveurs, nouvelle édition* (Paris: Librairie Gründ, 1948), 255.

41. Mardiros Artin (Harutun) Azadian to the Right Reverend Brown (ABCFM), December 1889 (according to the Julian Calendar), in Armenian. (Mardiros Artin was the father of H. B. Azadian.) Sachaklian Papers, Syracuse, New York.

42. Interview with Arshalouis Azadian Randall, 27 November 1966.

43. Ibid.

44. Ibid.; also corroborated by letters, photographs, passport information, and the personal and family memorandum book (Gedenkbuch) of Johanna and Hans (brother of Johanna) Zimmer. All manuscripts from the Johanna Zimmer Trust in Syracuse, N.Y., dating from 1857 to 1938, are fragmented but substantial. All Zimmer memorabilia unless otherwise stipulated is in the Azadian-Koolakian Papers.

45. Interview with Randall, 27 November 1966.

46. Interview with Randall, 27 November 1966; also corroborated by Dr. Antonie M. Kraut, an international lawyer from Stuttgart, Germany, in a letter to the author, 9 March 1967.

47. The Edison Pioneers was formally organized in New York City on 24 January 1918 by executive sanction of the Association of Edison Illuminating Companies (established in New York in 1885). Even before its formal organization in 1918, many of the Pioneers had become supporters of the ACASR, several having administrative status in that organization. Those involved included Dr. John W. Lieb, Preston S. and William B. Millar, Mary Pickford, John Sloane, William Sloane, Thomas Sloane, Jean Harlow, Lillian Russell, Ethel Barrymore, Anna Case, Torcom Bezazian, Edna White, Melville Clark, George Wilton Ballard, Fred Vare, Irving Kaufman, and Theda Bera, among many musicians and performing artists who staged benefits for the relief effort in cities and towns across the United States. Pioneer involvement in the administration of the NER program was evident especially in the regional New York and national committees of this organization.

48. When the Armenians were exiled from Banderma in August 1915, this then-elderly couple remarkably survived the Ottoman "death marches" to the Syrian desert and managed to seek the protection of the British High Relief Commission (under Lord James Bryce), which returned them to Constantinople and then arranged their passage to the United States from Constantinople in 1920.

49. The term "khunami" means a family member obtained through marriage, applied in this case to an "in-law" relationship between married members of the Azadian, Kechebashian, Koolakian, Danielian, Aghamalian, Altoonjian, Kelikian, Desteian, and Roomian families.

50. Interview with Leah Bayerian Armen, daughter of John Bayerian, 11 September 1991 in Syracuse, N.Y.

51. Evidenced by letters from George F. Hine regarding Harutun Azadian, 12 October 1899 to December 1903, Azadian-Koolakian Papers.

52. Affiliated with the ABCFM and the American Protestant mission movement in Constantinople, the Schmavonian family established themselves in nearby Cazenovia, N.Y., where Badvelli (Reverend) Arsene Schmavonian became resident pastor of a large Protestant congregation, and also served the Armenian Fourth Presbyterian Mission Church in Syracuse as a visiting minister for many years. During World War I, his brother, Arshag K. Schmavonian, served in the American embassy in Constantinople as a personal attaché to Ambassador Henry Morgenthau. The Schmavonians were well-known philanthropists in the United States, supporting Near East Relief and the Armenian Students' Association of America (established in Boston between 1909 and 1910).

53. Interview with Leah Bayerian Armen, 11 September 1991 in Syracuse, N.Y.

54. Corroborated by a review of names listed in consecutive volumes of *Boyd's Directory* (Syracuse, N.Y.: R. L. Polk and Co.). The directories were later published by Sampson and Murdock between 1895 and 1914.

55. Ibid. This was also corroborated by pre-1912 photographs taken of Armenians at the Beecher residence in Orwell, N.Y.

56. Haigazian and the others (except Azadian and Philibosian) had been close associates of Koolakian from the days of his youth at Banderma. Haigazian with his brother, Dr. Armenak Haigazian, became prominent supporters of the ABCFM and the later ACASR/NER. Well-known philanthropists, they later established Haigazian College (now Haigazian University), a recognized center of higher learning in the Middle East, at Beirut, Lebanon.

57. Dr. Yessaian, a prominent silk technologist from Banderma, later achieved fame in the United States as a distinguished entomologist (University of Southern California) after his move to San Clemente in the 1920s, becoming America's source for domestically cultured silk-farm supplies. Interestingly, Yessaian assisted Henry Ford in establishing the Hanks silk mill at his outdoor museum, Greenfield Village, following its dedication in 1929, and was an entomological supplier to that operation for many years.

58. Ernest J. Bowden, "Armenians Will Never Forget American Help, Pastor Says," *Syracuse Post-Standard*, 22 May 1939.

59. Corroborated by Syracuse newspaper accounts, correspondence, telegrams, and printed ACASR/NER campaign memorabilia, 1915–52, Azadian-

Koolakian Papers.

60. Dr. Robert Chambers, an officer with the ABCFM in Constantinople and a longtime friend of the Azadian family, was expelled from Turkey along with his colleague, the Reverend John H. Adjemian (the latter having been imprisoned), in the summer of 1915 on the pretext that they were Armenian sympathizers plotting to overthrow the Ottoman government. Chambers immediately returned to the United States, resuming his work for the ABCFM in Boston and in Syracuse. Adjemian was released later that summer through the direct diplomatic intervention of Ambassador Morgenthau. Adjemian, whose entire family had been killed during the 1915 Armenian massacres, was sent to Athens, Greece, where he taught for the ABCFM until 1938. Having previous ties to the central New York Armenian community, Adjemian then immigrated to Syracuse where he became resident minister of the Armenian Presbyterian Mission Church. He remained at that post until his death in 1952.

61. Also confirmed by Richard C. Robarts, president of the Near East Foundation in New York, in a letter to the author dated 14 February 1997.

62. "Armenians to Voice Protest on Massacres," *Syracuse Post-Standard*, 29 September 1915. In the weeks immediately following Ambassador Morgenthau's cable, there was considerable international coverage of the Armenian massacres in the Syracuse newspapers. Major articles appeared in the following issues of the *Syracuse Post-Standard:* 21 September 1915, 29 September 1915 (feature article), 30 September 1915, 4 October 1915 (front page), and 5 October 1915. A copy of the original Morgenthau cable was located in the archives of the Near East Foundation in New York City in 1997, thus confirming the provenance and source of George Koolakian's copy. Based upon the evidence, it can be concluded that Koolakian's copy was one of an unknown number that was transmitted by the ABCFM, Boston, to regional ABCFM-affiliated stations throughout the northeastern United States and elsewhere soon after the original was received by the state department.

63. "Armenians to Voice Protest on Massacres," from the *Syracuse Post-Standard*, 29 September 1915: "More than 250 Armenian residents of Syracuse plan to hold a mass meeting Sunday evening in the auditorium of the Fourth Presbyterian Church to voice through Americans as well as through themselves an unofficial appeal to Kaiser Wilhelm of Germany to halt the deportation and slaughter of their compatriots by the Turkish government."

64. Ibid.

65. *Armenia, "A Christian Nation": Her Heart-Rending Cry.*

66. Ibid.

67. "Armenians to Voice Protest on Massacres." See notes 62 and 63.

68. Correspondence and work reports, ACASR/NER, New York City, 1916–18, Azadian-Koolakian Papers.

69. Memorandum from Charles V. Vickrey, executive secretary of the ACASR/NER, New York City, to Syracuse coworkers, 21 October 1916, Azadian-Koolakian Papers. See Appendix 2 on pages 130, 131, and 132 for the three pages of the proclamation as passed by the Senate and signed by President Wilson.

70. Letter from Charles V. Vickrey, executive secretary of the ACASR/NER, New York City, to George Koolakian, Near East Relief, 22 January 1919, Azadian-Koolakian Papers.

71. Near East Foundation to the author, 14 February 1997.

72. "'Ravished Armenia' in Film: Mrs. Harriman Speaks at Showing of Turkish and German Devastation," *New York Times,* 15 February 1919.

73. Vickrey to Koolakian, 22 January 1919.

74. *Syracuse Post-Standard,* 9 September 1918, and chronicled in the diary of Arshalouis Azadian, 7–12 September 1919.

75. Diary of Arshalouis Azadian (later Randall), 12 September 1919.

76. Gregory Aftandilian, *Armenia, Vision of a Republic: The Independence Lobby in America, 1918–1927* (Boston: Charles River Books, 1981), 17.

77. James L. Barton, *The Story of Near East Relief: An Interpretation* (New York: Macmillan, 1930).

78. Writing about the American-Armenian independence movement, the prominent Armenian-American historian Richard G. Hovannisian states in *The Republic of Armenia* that "by intent, no Armenian American was invited to membership in the ACIA" (Berkeley and Los Angeles: University of California Press, 1971), 1:261, n. 34. However, it is readily proven that some were involved, if not as formal members. The Azadian-Koolakian family documents clearly indicate that certain well-established Armenians were, in fact, quietly chosen to participate as liaisons in the earliest activities of this organization in November and December of 1918 (see the telegram from William Jennings Bryan to George Koolakian of 8 January 1919). This heretofore "unknown list" of Amenian Americans without question included Harutun Azadian, George Koolakian, and Harry P. Philibosian, who are documented as having taken part in the advance planning and direct participation in the ACIA's founding convention on the weekend of 7 and 8 February 1919. An executive committee member of the ABCFM, the ACASR/NER, and the ACIA, James L. Barton offers a plausible explanation as to why few Armenians were involved: "The

Armenians present at some of the earlier meetings gave valuable information about the situation and need in Turkey, obtained by them through independent sources. It was decided, however, that as they were the people chiefly involved [affected], they should not be made members of the Committee, which should be an all-American body, non-political and absolutely neutral (*The Story of Near East Relief,* 14, n. 2). It is evident that this organizational philosophy, which was employed in the formation of the ACASR/NER, was also carried forward into the charter ACIA organization upon its formation in November and December of 1918 and during its first convention meetings held in Manhattan on 7, 8, and 9 February of 1919 by those concurrent interorganizational trustees who were serving both organizations, including Barton, himself.

79. Many of Cardashian's papers were published in volumes 10 (nos. 1–37) and 11 (nos. 3–43) (Spring 1957 and Autumn 1958) of the *Armenian Review,* among other places.

80. Letter of Dr. James H. Tashjian to the author, 12 February 1996.

81. Letter from Charles V. Vickrey to James R. Day, cofounder of the Syracuse branch of the ACASR, 17 November 1918, Azadian-Koolakian Papers (courtesy of Arshalouis Azadian Randall).

82. Link, *Papers of Woodrow Wilson,* 41:217.

83. The message in this telegram was preceded by a discussion that included New York State Assembly leader Thaddeus C. Sweet, Theodore Roosevelt, and Elihu Root. This fact is confirmed in a letter from Sweet to Koolakian, written from the Masonic Lodge in Syracuse on 2 December 1918. All of them were supporters of the NER campaign. Sweet, who was elected to the New York State Legislature in 1909, was a Syracuse Masonic Lodge brother with Azadian, Koolakian, and Philibosian for many years, and a longtime friend of Theodore Roosevelt. Sweet attended the first ACIA convention at the Hotel Plaza in New York and played a role in the early Armenian independence movement. He may have been instrumental in the earlier introduction of Azadian, Koolakian, and Philibosian to Theodore Roosevelt and his family.

84. Koolakian kept Roosevelt family memorabilia, including an original first edition of *Theodore Roosevelt, Patriot and Statesman: The True Story of an Ideal American* (Philadelphia: P. W. Ziegler and Co., 1902) published privately by author Robert C. Meyers, which Roosevelt autographed for Koolakian in 1912. Most likely, Koolakian had had contact with him during his prior term of office. When he came to the U.S. in 1905, Koolakian was already an admirer of Roosevelt.

85. Theodore Roosevelt was posthumously recognized by James L. Barton of the ABCFM as one of the foremost organizers of the New York State

ACASR/NER program upon its inception in September 1915. Roosevelt's outstanding record of contribution was subsequently written into the record of the NER upon its incorporation by Congressional proclamation on 6 August 1919. (See Barton, *Story of Near East Relief*.)

86. Thomas Edison was the founding organizer and honorary president of the United States Naval Consulting Board, having a close affiliation with naval secretary Josephus Daniels, the first chairman of the NCB.

87. The Sloanes were prominent New York entrepreneurs, having family ties in New York City and in New Jersey. Affiliated with the ABCFM for many years, the Sloanes served in various administrative positions, ultimately being named to the board of directors. William Sloane (son of the prominent John Sloane) became a director of Robert College in Constantinople, serving in that post for a number of years prior to World War I. During the war, he became chairman of the Committee on Work for Allied Armies and Prisoners of War, which was affiliated with the YMCA and its international secretary, John Mott. Sloane oversaw their work inspections throughout the European front. Soon after the formation of the ACASR/NER in 1915, Sloane became a trustee, serving in that organization until his death in 1922. The younger John E. Sloane married Madeleine Edison, daughter of the inventor, in 1914.

88. Evidenced by a sectional closeup photograph showing the head table, 8 February 1919, Hotel Plaza, New York, Azadian-Koolakian Papers.

89. Roster of the ACASR/NER "New York Officers" and "Members of the New York Committee," New York, October 1917, Azadian-Koolakian Papers.

90. The existence of Charles Stewart Davison's state department memorandum dated 7 February 1919 and its citation of his 20 January 1919 telegram to Woodrow Wilson more clearly establishes the provenance of the original membership roster of the ACIA. The above state department telegram referencing the January 1919 petitioners of the ACIA establishes Davison by this time as the vice chairman of the new organization, whereas the prior ACIA roster includes him only on the general committee. Therefore, Davison's recent appointment as the ACIA vice chairman early in 1919 places him as one of the chief organizers of the inaugural convention held between 7 and 11 February 1919.

91. Corroborated in part in the personal diary of Arshalouis Azadian, 7 February 1919. Philibosian was already in New York at this time.

92. "City Gives Million to Armenian Relief," *New York Times*, 8 February 1919.

93. Ibid.

94. See the telegram from James W. Gerard to Azadian and Koolakian of 4

February 1919, fig. 43 on page 90.

95. *Moving Picture World* (40 [no. 9] for 31 May 1919). A broadside for the motion picture *Armenia Ravished* appears in this publication, indicating also that Charles W. Eliot (president emeritus of Harvard University, a supporter of the ABCFM and the ACASR/NER, and an officer in the ACIA), played a part in supporting the production of this film. Although the press failed to acknowledge George Eastman's presence at the ACIA convention, the Koolakian papers include another telegram from Eastman to Koolakian dated 4 February 1919: "Note change unable to stop in Syracuse on trip to New York kindly bring finished garments in hand to Hotel Plaza need Saturday night join you and Azadians upon arrival many thanks."

96. "'Ravished Armenia' in Film"; "Show 'Ravished Armenia': First Public Exhibition of Official Motion Picture Today," *New York Times,* 17 February 1919.

97. Ibid.

98. It is likely that these telegrams were among the international messages that were acknowledged and read to the attendees at the ACIA's convention banquet the following evening. It has also been suggested that the first two messages were transmitted with the full knowledge and imprimatur of the state department, if not sent directly from them. This hypothesis is supported not only by their context but also by the wording in the (third) telegram from Charles Steinmetz giving specific reference to Azadian and Koolakian's recognized status with the American delegation and the ACIA.

99. The telegram is signed by Woodrow Wilson, indicating that these men probably had a later meeting with him, or it was possibly taken in person by Wilson's wife (who attended the 8 February inaugural) and returned to Azadian and Koolakian at a later date.

100. Writing about the Armenian independence movement, the prominent Armenian American historian Richard G. Hovannisian states that "by intent, no Armenian American was invited to membership in the ACIA" (*The Republic of Armenia, Volume I: The First Year, 1918–1919* [Berkeley and Los Angeles: University of California Press, 1971], 261, n. 34). However, the Azadian-Koolakian family documents prove that a few well-established Armenians were in fact quietly chosen to participate as liaisons in the organization from its inception between November and December 1918. This heretofore "unknown list" of Armenian Americans included Harutun Azadian, George Koolakian, and Harry Philibosian, who helped plan and participated in the ACIA's founding convention beginning the weekend of 7 and 8 February 1919. An executive committee member of the ABCFM, the ACASR/NER, and the ACIA, Dr. James L. Barton offers a plausible explanation as to why few Armenians were involved: "The Armenians present at some of

the earlier meetings gave valuable information about the situation and need in Turkey, obtained by them through independent sources. It was decided, however, that as they were the people chiefly involved [affected], they should not be made members of the Committee, which should be an all-American body, non-political and absolutely neutral" (Barton, *Story of Near East Relief,* 14, n. 2). This organizational philosophy had also applied to the formation of the ACASR/NER.

101. "New Amendments Forecast by Bryan; Predicts Initiative and Referendum Will Be Part of Constitution; Wants Armenia Freed; Charles E. Hughes Also Urges This, but Opposes U.S. Protectorate," *New York Sun,* 9 February 1919.

102. Confirmed by "The Plaza Historian" in a letter to the author dated 6 August 1996.

103. Vickrey to Koolakian, 22 January 1919.

104. See the photograph "Banquet of the American Committee for Armenian Independence Hotel Plaza N.Y. February 8, 1919," Azadian-Koolakian Papers, and Aftandilian, *Armenia, Vision of a Republic,* 28.

105. Concerning the identification of numbers 17 and 20 as being Baron Nobuaki Makino and Chonosuke Yada, Baron Makino was a newly recognized member of the Paris Peace Conference, having been appointed to its Supreme Allied Council, the peace conference decision-making body composed of the heads of government and foreign ministers of the United States, Great Britain, France, Italy, and Japan.

106. The term used at that time for what is now called the "Diocese of the Armenian Church of America (Eastern)."

107. Morton had served as the twenty-second vice president of the United States (1889–93) under Benjamin Harrison, and as minister (the equivalent of ambassador) to France during the administrations of James Garfield and Chester Arthur (1881–85). Morton and his family had important historical connections to the ABCFM, his father having been a Congregational minister with the American Board in the Ottoman Empire, and his uncle, Levi Parsons Morton (for whom he was named), having been appointed the first American missionary to the Ottoman Empire to serve in Palestine. During the Civil War, Morton founded the well-known Wall Street banking house of L. P. Morton and Company that ultimately became known as Morton Bliss and Company. Morton's partner, George Parsons Bliss (a relative on his mother's side), was a member of the prominent Bliss family, also having close early connections with the ABCFM (Boston and New York), whose later contemporaries (General Tasker Bliss and Dr. Edwin W. Bliss) also served as advisors to the Paris Peace Conference and the Armenian independence movement. The

partnership of Morton Bliss and Company became one of America's leading banking establishments, having connections to Abraham Lincoln's presidency. Morton's British operation, Morton Rose and Company in London was appointed a financial agent to the United States government in 1873. Morton and his two firms became pioneer philanthropists in the founding of Robert College in Constantinople under Dr. Cyrus Hamlin and John Sloane of the ABCFM. Having established his fortune, Morton turned to public service, first as a congressman representing New York's eleventh district from 1879 to 1881, being reelected in 1880 by one vote against his opponent, James Watson Gerard Jr. (later ambassador to Germany, founding chairman of the ACIA, and comaster of ceremonies of the inaugural banquet), then serving in the above-mentioned offices in the 1880s and early 1890s, and becoming governor of New York State in 1894. From 1894 to 1896, Morton extended his philanthropic work by initiating and organizing the collection and distribution of considerable humanitarian relief to victims of the Hamidian massacres in the Ottoman Empire, via his associate William Wheelock Peet, treasurer of the ABCFM in Constantinople, a prelude to Morton's extended philanthropic work during the Armenian genocide in his support of the ACASR/NER effort. In 1909, Morton's American firm (Morton Bliss and Company) merged with Morgan Guaranty Trust Company. Morton remained active until his death on his ninety-sixth birthday, 16 May 1920, a year and one-half after participating in the founding activities of the Armenian independence movement. An exemplary man of financial and international affairs, Morton was a member of many public-spirited organizations, including the New York State Grand Masonic Lodge, a post he held with Theodore Roosevelt.

108. In documenting and describing the atrocities against Armenians late in 1915, the ACASR campaign used the term "extermination," and wrote that "this process of wiping out an entire people is more cruel and abhorrent than any massacre which modern history records." Azadian-Koolakian Papers.

109. "Hughes Joins Bryan in Plea for Armenia," unidentified article (possibly the *New York American*), 9 February 1919. Additional coverage of this event includes "Free Armenia Is Plea of Hughes," *World Sunday* (New York), 9 February 1919; "Hughes and Bryan Join in Plea for Armenian Nation," *New York Herald*, 9 February 1919; and "New Amendments Forecast by Bryan," *Sun* (New York), 9 February 1919.

110. "Hughes Joins Bryan in Plea for Armenia," clipping from unidentified newspaper, 9 February 1919, Azadian-Koolakian Papers.

111. Ibid.

112. Ibid.

113. One contemporary account gives the number of Armenians in the United States in 1919 as 77,980 (M. Vartan Malcom, *The Armenians in America*

[Boston: Pilgrim Press, 1919], 67), while a modern scholar has calculated the number of Armenians who emigrated to the United States by the end of 1914 as 65,950 (Robert Mirak, *Torn between Two Lands: Armenians in America, 1890 to World War I* [Cambridge: Harvard University Press, 1983], 290).

114. "Hughes Joins Bryan in Plea for Armenia." See also: "Free Armenia Is Plea of Hughes," *New York World*, 9 February 1919; "Hughes and Bryan Join in Plea for Armenian Nation," *New York Herald*, 9 February 1919; and "New Amendments Forecast by Bryan," *New York Sun*, 9 February 1919.

115. "Internal Communication," from C. V. V. (Charles V. Vickrey) to the ACIA Banquet Planning Committee, 22 January 1919.

116. Wilson to Azadian and Koolakian, 7 February 1919 (see fig. 55 on page 111).

117. His remarks were incorporated into his *The Armenians in America* (Boston: Pilgrim Press, 1919), 34–35, which was published a few months later.

118. "Internal Communication," 22 January 1919. A description of the banquet was published in Boston on the front page of the Armenian-language daily *Hayrenik* (Fatherland), on 14 February 1919. Under the header "Patmakan Havakoyt Me" (A Historic Gathering), it mentions that Gerard did, indeed, introduce Hughes and Bryan, who spoke for forty and forty-five minutes, respectively. In between their speeches, de Treville did sing Warford's "Armenia." Mihran Sivasly spoke on behalf of the Armenian National Delegation, which had been formed by the head of the Armenian Church in the aftermath of the Balkan Wars of 1912 and 1913. Messages of support were read from the French, British, Italian, Greek, and Romanian governments.

119. Diary of Arshalouis Azadian, 11 February 1919, Azadian-Koolakian Papers.

120. "Woodrow Wilson," *Funk and Wagnall's Standard Encyclopedia* (New York: Standard Reference Works Publishing Co., 1964), 25:9226.

121. Elisabeth Bauer, *Armenia: Past and Present,* trans. by Frederick A. Leist (New York: Armenian Prelacy, 1981), 148–49.

This book incorporates material from German, Russian, Armenian, and English sources spanning three centuries; as a result, several alternate forms of names are employed in the text. A'Zad, Zaduni, and Azadoff are alternate forms of the modern Azadian. Artin and Artemy are diminutives of Harutun. Artemjeff and Ardemitz are alternate forms of Artjemeff. Negale and Nicolai are Armenian and Russian forms, respectively, of the same name. Page numbers that are followed by the letter *f* signify figures or captions for figures on those pages.

Robert George Koolakian is a native of Syracuse, New York, and a 1966 alumnus of Syracuse University. He received a graduate degree in historical methodology and history museum procedures through the State University of New York. In Michigan, he held curatorial and administrative positions at the Henry Ford Museum in Dearborn, and he taught courses in museology at Oakland University. In central New York, he served as director of the Erie Canal Museum and has been involved in various museum and historic preservation projects. Widely regarded as one of the foremost authorities on the life and works of Thomas Alva Edison, Koolakian helped organize the Syracuse University Audio Archives and Edison Re-recording Laboratory, and worked with its director on the development of techniques in the recovery and preservation of early recorded sound. Koolakian has many position papers, articles, and books to his credit, and has lectured widely in the United States.

Colophon

The text of this volume was edited by Mary Beth Hinton. The book was designed in InDesign cs3 by William T. La Moy and composed entirely in Adobe Caslon, an OpenType font that Carol Twombly created for Adobe based upon her scrutiny of William Caslon's type specimens produced between 1734 and 1770. The paper for the text is Mead's Moistrite Matte in a weight of seventy pounds. Michelle Combs provided the index. The book publishing consultant was Alice Nigoghosian.